BEA ROBERTS

Bea Roberts is a multi-award-winning playwright and screenwriter from the West Country. Her debut play, *And Then Come The Nightjars*, won the Theatre503 International Playwriting Award, made her a finalist for the prestigious Susan Smith Blackburn Prize, and was adapted into a feature film with Finite Pictures.

Her next project, the one-woman/no-woman show *Infinity Pool: A Modern Retelling of Madame Bovary* had a sell-out run at the Edinburgh Festival, was nominated for a Total Theatre award and was optioned by Hartswood Films. Bea's modern feminist adaptation of *Little Mermaid* won Best Play for Children & Young People at the 2018 UK Theatre Awards. Other writing credits include *Ivy Tiller: Vicar's Daughter, Squirrel Killer* (Royal Shakespeare Company), utopian eco-comedy *Loam* (Royal Welsh College of Music and Drama in association with the Royal Court), and *Sir F. Mother****ing Drake* starring *Fleabag*'s Jenny Rainsford, part of the *My England* monologue series at the Young Vic. She was shortlisted for the International George Devine Playwriting Award in 2023.

Bea was selected for BBC Studio's Writers' Academy in 2022 and became a writer on the BBC's flagship soap *EastEnders*. She currently has new work in development across stage and screen.

Other Titles in this Series

Bea Roberts

THE WHITBY REBELS

NICK HERN BOOKS

London

www.nickhernbooks.co.uk

A Nick Hern Book

The Whitby Rebels first published in Great Britain in 2024 as a paperback original by Nick Hern Books Limited, The Glasshouse, 49a Goldhawk Road, London W12 8QP

The Whitby Rebels copyright © 2024 Bea Roberts

Bea Roberts has asserted her right to be identified as the author of this work

Front cover: photography by Drew Forsyth; design by Rebecca Pitt

Designed and typeset by Nick Hern Books, London
Printed in Great Britain by Mimeo Ltd, Huntingdon, Cambridgeshire PE29 6XX

A CIP catalogue record for this book is available from the British Library

ISBN 978 1 83904 397 0

www.nickhernbooks.co.uk/environmental-policy

The Whitby Rebels was first performed at the Stephen Joseph Theatre, Scarborough, on 18 October 2024, with the following cast:

CAPTAIN JACK LAMMIMAN	Keith Bartlett
EDNA WHELAN	Jacky Naylor
PAT STUBBS	Jacqueline King
REVEREND PAUL BURKITT	Duncan MacInnes
LEWIS TURNBULL/	Kieran Foster
PUB BLOKE	
SUNNY/OTHERS	Louise Mai Newberry

Director	Paul Robinson
Designer	Jessica Curtis
Lighting Designer	Sally Ferguson
Composer and Sound Designer	Simon Slater
Movement Director	Georgina Lamb
Wardrobe Supervisor	Julia Perry-Mook
Fight Director	Kaitlin Howard
Nautical Consultant	Tom Hill
Casting Director	Sarah Hughes CDG
Production Manager	Simon Bedwell
Technical Manager	Mark 'Tigger' Johnson
Set Construction	Topshow
Scenic Artists	Joanne and Nigel Ellis, Julia Wray
Company Stage Manager	Fleur Linden Beeley
Deputy Stage Manager	Steve Muckersie
Assistant Stage Manager	Phoebe Storm

The Whitby Rebels was commissioned by the Stephen Joseph Theatre in 2020.

Acknowledgements

Particular thanks must go to Paul Burkitt and Rosemary Redway for so generously sharing their time and trusting us with their stories; I hope we've done you proud. Thanks to the Skipper, Paul Robinson, for getting me on board and to all the crew at the Stephen Joseph for steering this play through a global pandemic.

Thanks to my brilliant agent, Jessica Cooper, and my wonderful husband, Luke Haines, may we always carry Paul's melody with us – 'an insatiable faith in life'.

B.R.

This play is inspired by and dedicated to the adventurous souls who sailed aboard the Helga Maria: *the Reverend Paul Burkitt, Edna Whelan, Pat Stubbs, Rosemary Redway, Dave Gray, Eric Smith, Captain Jack Lammiman, and many others.*

Characters

CAPTAIN JACK LAMMIMAN, *male, sixties. White. From Whitby. Enigmatic, roguish, softly spoken*
EDNA WHELAN, *female, seventies. White. From Yorkshire. Romantic, wistful, poetic, steely*
PAT STUBBS, *female, seventies. White. RP. Seemingly unflappable, competent, reserved*
REVEREND PAUL BURKITT, *male, forties. White. From Hull. Spiritual, well travelled, independent*
LEWIS TURNBULL, *male, twenties–thirties. West Indies heritage. Scouser. Outspoken, practical, blokey, mischievous*
SUNNY, *female, thirties–fifties. South East Asian heritage. From Yorkshire. Jack's secretary, international diplomatic liaison and caravan-park worker*
CAPTAIN BRENDA McCAWLEE, *Scottish, from the Department of Transport. Professional, dry humour*
FRANK, *Scottish, Jack's sailing friend, very drunk*

And PUB BLOKE, A WIDOW, RADIO HOST, PARISHIONER, NORWEGIAN SCIENTIST, THE PRESS, MAGISTRATE

Doubling

This play is for a cast of six actors playing multiple roles:

The actor playing LEWIS *also plays* PUB BLOKE.

The actor playing SUNNY *also plays* CAPTAIN McCAWLEE, FRANK, WIDOW, PARISHONER, NORWEGIAN SCIENTIST.

MAGISTRATE, RADIO HOST *and* THE PRESS *may be pre-recorded by the cast.*

Setting

The action of the play takes place between 1991 and the present day, between Whitby and the Arctic Circle. Locations include 1960s' schooner the *Helga Maria*, Whitby Harbour, the islands of Foula and Jan Mayen, a caravan park, a magistrates' court and the ocean; mostly the ocean.

Note on Text

In the script, punctuation is used to denote rhythm and emphasis of dialogue.

A dash (–) on its own line indicates a pause or beat; or, at the end of a line, a character cut off or stopping mid-sentence.

A forward slash (/) indicates where the next character begins speaking, interrupting dialogue.

[Square brackets] indicate a word that was meant but not said.

Note on Play

This story is a dramatisation inspired by real-life voyages; certain characters, scenes and events have been invented for dramatic purposes. The play draws on text taken from the recordings, interviews and accounts of Paul Burkitt and Rosemary Redway as well as Edna Whelan's book *The Helga Maria* and contemporary press coverage.

This text went to press before the end of rehearsals and so may differ slightly from the play as performed.

Prologue

The sound of a heavy ocean swell then other sounds swim in and wash out: radio static, clogs walking across a wooden deck, high winds, paparazzi. A story is surfacing from the depths of the ocean. Sounds of the nineties swim in and out then 'Get Ready for This' by 2 Unlimited.

Lights criss-cross and dance. It's big and bombastic. Suddenly the music cuts out, leaving SUNNY *raving in a spotlight with her clipboard. The sudden focus makes her jump –*

SUNNY. Oh jeez – nearly give me an heart attack that did! Sorry everyone. 'Good evening! I'm – ' Nah – that's put me right off me stride.

SUNNY *shouts up to the tech desk.*

Let me take it again. Leave me light on. Sorry. I'll get it on second try. Go again.

'Get Ready for This' by 2 Unlimited blasts out. Lights criss-cross and dance. SUNNY *tries to gauge the right moment to jump in with her narration. She's wrong a couple of times.*

Finally –

Good evening Scarborough! Yeah, that's the one. My name is Sunny and I've got some notices before we begin tonight's entertainment! Cos all the best shows start with a disclaimer don't they?! Right –

(*Consults her clipboard.*) It's an author's note, which it's specified int script *I'm* to read out. So, you know –

SUNNY *preens.*

I may be but a small cog within this story but evidently they needed someone with star power, someone oozing charisma, someone who's not needed in the next scene and available to read this. Anyroad, this author says here 'In July of 1991 the *Helga Maria* set sail from Whitby Harbour bound for the Arctic island of Jan Mayen. What happened on that fateful voyage was to become the stuff of myth and movies and tabloids that soon became chip paper but *what really happened?*' And she's done that bit all in italics for emphasis '*What really happened?*'

'Like with most great stories that all depends on who you ask. What follows is a dramatisation, certain characters and events' blah blah blah, just gonna paraphrase.

...Alright, yeah, basically a lot of this story's true but some of it's cobblers.

Okay, best get on with it then. 'Our story begins in Whitby in the year 1992!' No it dunt, I were there. Started in '91 didn't it?

Projection: '1992.'

Projection: 'Whitby Magistrates' Court.'

Oh it's a *flash-forward*, that's fancy int it?!

The crack of a gavel. SUNNY *starts to scuttle offstage.*

Wait, I'm not in this bit!

SUNNY *exits.*

CAPTAIN JACK LAMMIMAN *stands in the dock in an ill-fitting second-hand suit. He stands upright, staring ahead, holding himself stiffly as if he's a marble statue. We may see the* MAGISTRATE *or they could be a voice-over.*

MAGISTRATE. Mr Lammiman, you stand accused of forty-three separate offences as detailed under the Merchant Shipping Act including sailing in defiance of a detention order, sailing in a vessel deemed unfit for purpose and unlawful transportation of civilian passengers into international waters causing danger to life. Do you have anything you'd like to say to the court Mr Lammiman?

JACK *stands implacable, inscrutable.*

Mr Lammiman?

JACK *looks squarely at the bench. Smiles...*

JACK. It's 'Captain Lammiman' all folk know that. 'Captain. Jack.'

'The One and Only' by Chesney Hawkes. We go back to 1991.

ACT ONE

Scene One

Detention Order

Projection: 'Whitby Harbour, 1991.'

It's a bright summer's morning. We hear the sound of seagulls and the gentle clanking of the halliards as boats bob on their moorings. The Helga Maria *is moored to the harbour wall.*

CAPTAIN BRENDA McCAWLEE *is inspecting the boat;* JACK *tails her, anxiously smoking a pipe.*

BRENDA. Hmmmmm.

> BRENDA *makes a note on her clipboard,* JACK *peers over her shoulder.*

JACK. What was that?

> BRENDA *wafts pipe smoke out of her face with obvious annoyance.*

BRENDA. Beg your pardon?

JACK. You said something.

BRENDA. I did not.

JACK. There was an utterance.

BRENDA. I uttered nothing Mr / Lammiman.

JACK. You 'hmm'd'.

BRENDA. And?

JACK. Well, I'm just trying to ascertain whether that was an 'everything's shipshape – hmm' or a 'that's going to be very expensive – hmm'.

BRENDA. Mr Lammiman I wasn't even aware I'd 'hmm'd'.

> BRENDA *gets out a tape measure to measure the bell.* JACK *rings it loudly;* BRENDA *does not appreciate this.*

JACK. It works.

BRENDA. Evidently. But it must still be measured to check it's / regulation size.

JACK. 'Regulation' yes I know.

BRENDA indicates for JACK to move out of the way of the bell.

BRENDA. If you would?

JACK moves a little. BRENDA indicates for him to move further back. JACK does. BRENDA indicates for him to move further back again.

JACK. Any further back I'll be off the boat and in the harbour!

BRENDA. Also an option. If you'd prefer to wait elsewhere.

EDNA WHELAN interrupts, walking along the harbour wall with her paints and easel.

EDNA. Coooooooee! Glorious morning Jack!

JACK. Morning Edna.

EDNA. I just had to capture the light, if only Titian had ever made it to Whitby! Oooh who's your friend?

JACK. Department of Transport.

JACK mimes pushing BRENDA off the boat and into the water.

EDNA. Well I have the upmost confidence Jack, it'll be five stars or whatever you use. Ten out of ten! You'll not find a finer vessel than the *Helga Maria*!

BRENDA has tuned out EDNA.

Excuse me, Mrs Transport Office?

BRENDA. That's 'Captain McCawlee'.

EDNA. I said you'll not find a finer vessel than the *Helga Maria*.

BRENDA. Hmm.

JACK. See there, you just 'hmm'd again.

BRENDA. Hmm?

JACK. Well now you're just doing it on purpose.

BRENDA *taps the bell.*

BRENDA. This is two centimetres too small.

EDNA. For what?

BRENDA. The regulations stipulated by the Department of Transport.

JACK. Come come now, as if another boat would hear this sounding in the ocean and think 'well it sounds like a vessel but it can't be because it sounds two millimetres –

BRENDA. Centimetres –

JACK. too small!'

EDNA. Surely it's not the size of the bell it's the size of the dong?!

–

BRENDA. I am not here to argue with you Mr Lammiman, I am here to –

JACK. Nitpick more's the pity.

BRENDA. Keep you safe.

EDNA. Would a bigger clacker help?

EDNA *clambers aboard.*

Within the casing? A bigger clacker would surely lead to a more resonant dong?

–

BRENDA. No.

Reads from her clipboard.

You need tape on the life jackets –

JACK. There is tape –

BRENDA. It's frayed. New tape. New fire extinguishers and flares. Six regulation fire buckets inclusive of but not limited to three for sand, three for water. A door between midships cabin and the / forrard –

JACK. Mark this Edna, there is no door between midships cabin and forrard –

BRENDA. Exactly, Mr Lammiman. There isn't and there should be. In case of fire.

EDNA. Surely you'd jump overboard if there were a fire on a boat?!

BRENDA. Not if you're trapped in the midships cabin due to lack of a door, madam. Mr Lammiman, I had hoped you would have implemented more of our recommendations, I thought I had impressed upon you the importance... I'm left with no choice –

BRENDA *hands* JACK *several forms and disembarks.*

JACK. A detention order?!

BRENDA. These are legal safety requirements not mere suggestions. Attend to these in full and then we'll need to re-inspect before your travels –

JACK. You're banning me from sailing for some fire buckets and whatnot?!

EDNA. We're going to the Arctic you know! I, for one, am not too fussed about fire!

BRENDA. You're part of the crew, madam?

JACK *waves to* EDNA, *trying to signal 'no'.* EDNA *misinterprets this and gives* JACK *a salute.*

EDNA. Oh yes, Able Seaman, Seawoman, Edna Whelan!

BRENDA *climbs back aboard watching* EDNA *like a hawk.*

BRENDA. You have much sailing experience Mrs Whelan?

EDNA. Indeed, we had the loveliest day trip to Scarborough –

JACK *tries to signal to* EDNA *'further'.*

– seden in Sweden.

BRENDA. 'Scarboroughseden'?

EDNA. In Sweden. Yes. Lovely it was.

BRENDA. You sailed to Sweden and back in a day?

EDNA.... we were very lucky with the wind.

–

JACK. Thank you for your diligence Captain McCawlee –

BRENDA. What position do you intend to take on this Arctic voyage Mrs Whelan?

EDNA. Oooh, I'd say standing up when it's nice, sitting down when it's windy!

JACK. We do cherish Edna's sense of humour –

BRENDA. So am I right in thinking, Mrs Whelan, that you won't be the qualified master or one of the three deck officers that are legally required to be part of the crew on a journey into international waters?

EDNA. Not in a manner of speaking –

BRENDA. So what will your duties be within the crew?

EDNA. Well / I can –

JACK. We've yet to tackle exact / roles –

BRENDA. I addressed the question to Mrs Whelan and she seems more than capable of answering for herself. Please do go on.

EDNA. As I was saying I can turn my hand to all sorts.

JACK *relaxes, that doesn't seem too bad.*

But I imagine my official capacity will be the officer for morale and light entertainment! It's a jolly long way to the Arctic and the last thing we'll be needing is people going round with faces like a wet Wednesday in Wakefield! Now I appreciate you have a job to do but I must say, is this so very necessary?! They didn't have health and safety gumpf like this in the days of William Scoresby – who this very pilgrimage we will shortly undertake is to honour! Put that on your clipboard missus! When Scoresby and his crew set out to charter unknown lands did they think 'oh we best not lads, cos that rope's got a frayed bit and that clacker's two inches too small'. No, they did not!

Now I may not have your fancy naval qualifications but I have a fine head filled with common sense, common sense that is sadly in short supply at many government agencies today, and I know to get out of the way of a fire and that when one travels by boat the only rule that really matters is to stay out of the wet bit!

–

BRENDA. Mr Lammiman would you face the stern please.

JACK *wearily does so.*

Mrs Whelan, could you point to starboard for me, please?

EDNA. Everyone knows the starboard side is the right side.

BRENDA *looks up and down the boat alternately facing the stern and the bow.*

BRENDA. Which right side?

EDNA.…the boat's.

BRENDA *disembarks.*

BRENDA. Call the office when you've got a full crew list and you've carried out the necessary repairs Mr Lammiman.

JACK. And how am I supposed to get anything to make repairs when I'm not allowed to leave the harbour?

BRENDA. Catch a bus?

BRENDA *goes to leave and then turns back.*

It is a jolly long way to the Arctic Mrs Whelan. Much longer than that day trip you took to Sweden. That's why we need to make sure the vessel you sail in is safe and up to code. Thousands of people die every year because they go in the wet bit.

BRENDA *exits.* EDNA *nudges* JACK *in triumph.*

EDNA. Well that's her told.

Scene Two

Jolly Sailors

Later. The Jolly Sailors Pub in Whitby. A buzzy Friday evening.
JACK is holding court, the centre of attention, king of the pub
anecdote, talking to EDNA and PUB BLOKE. Some way
through this, REVEREND PAUL BURKITT weaves his way
over to JACK, carefully carrying two pints.

JACK. So, I think to myself, 'Jacky boy, there is no way you're
getting down that corridor, past them guards, in *clogs*' right?!
Wake the whole cell block. So I've a clog stuffed up each
shirtsleeve, looking like Popeye's biceps, but that's no bad
thing you run into trouble! Maybe they'll take one look and
think twice! So...

JACK pauses for dramatic effect.

...the lock's picked, thank you Sister Catalina for the
hairpin. The door swings open – on rusty hinges with
a creeeeak I will never forget.

I wait. But not a guard stirs from the office up the corridor.

I put one foot, barefoot, out the cell – but of course, 'el sol
Marroc' has been streaming through the skylights, heating up
the terracotta tile nigh on sixteen hours! I step out – *I heard my*
own skin sizzle, no – I did! Talk about 'little piggies' my right
foot is cooking like bacon so I am literally hotstepping it –

PAUL arrives, interrupting with a pint.

Thank you Paul. Hotstepping it –

PAUL. What have I missed?

EDNA. Jack's daring escape from a Moroccan prison!

PAUL. I thought it was a Spanish prison?

PUB BLOKE. 'Algeria' you said?

JACK. Ah, well...

EDNA. So, you've picked the lock but the terracotta's burning
hot –

JACK. I've rather lost my thread now. Cheers, anyroad.

PAUL. Sorry, yes, cheers to your last night on dry land!

EDNA. Pardon?

PAUL. Jack's setting sail for the Arctic!

PUB BLOKE. Are ya?!

EDNA. Not without me he isn't and I've not made
arrangements for the cat! We're not going tomorrow, Jack?!

JACK. No, not tomorrow exactly...

PAUL (*senses something's up*). Oh?

JACK. But... it'll not be long. I'll check the tides.

PAUL. Well. It's going to be such an adventure, I'm rather
envious.

PUB BLOKE. What you goin' to t'Arctic for?

EDNA. A pilgrimage. A rather sacred one, if I do say, to honour
oft-and-unfairly-overlooked Whitby hero Captain William
Scoresby! Inventor of the crow's nest, discoverer of
unknown lands.

There's a whole flotilla of us following in his footsteps, well
sailing in his... watery... path? Anyway it's gonna be like an
armada voyaging to the island of Jan Mayen, isn't that right
Jack?

JACK *nods...*

PAUL. So exciting!

EDNA. I'm getting a hat! It'll be in all the papers.

PUB BLOKE (*to* EDNA, *incredulous*). You're going an' all?

EDNA (*defensive, regal*). Yes. It'll be in all the papers. I'm
getting a hat.

PAUL. I'm so happy it's come together for you.

PUB BLOKE. Ay. Fair play to ya!

JACK. There's uh, still room, for crew if you're game? Can
always use an able seaman! Both of you? Come on. Sailing
into polar seas like our forefathers of old, riding the open
waves side by side with dolphins and blue whales. Just the salt

and spray and endless horizon, stretching out before you – and all yours for the taking. It's the trip of a lifetime!

PAUL. I wish I could!

PUB BLOKE. Not me. I once got sick on a pedalo.
Peasholm Park.
Ruined my mother's espadrilles.

They're interrupted as SUNNY *rushes over in a wedding veil, a lurid-colour cocktail in one hand, a camera in the other. She's a little tipsy –*

SUNNY. There he is! Let's get a photo of the conquering hero!

SUNNY *hands* PAUL *her cocktail.*

Take this a sec would ya, in fact, have it if you like, it's horrible. Gordon reckons it's a Sex on the Beach, I said 'Gordon, Sex on the Beach?! More like a fumble on a towpath!' Oops sorry vicar!

PAUL *laughs away the suggestion,* SUNNY *points her camera at* JACK.

Say 'iceberg'!

JACK. No.

SUNNY. I am taking a photo in three seconds regardless of if you're smiling. One – two – three!

Snap!

Well you're gonna be sorry when I send that in to t'paper! Oh come here.

SUNNY *swoops in, hugging* JACK; EDNA *bristles.*

JACK. It's a very fetching veil but I'm not marrying you Sunny.

SUNNY. Oh go on, Paul's right here, come on vicar!

PAUL. Let me get my cassock!

SUNNY. Ay, you should be so lucky Captain Jack! You daftie, we're out for our Jazz's hen do.

EDNA *peers imperiously across the bar.*

EDNA. Which one's the bride? The one with back tattoos or the one waggling the inflatable... doodah.

SUNNY *looks over, unfazed.*

SUNNY. Doodah.

–

EDNA. Would you excuse me gentlemen? I see an acquaintance of mine from intermediate ceramics.

EDNA *exits.*

SUNNY (*calls after her, amused*). Ay Edna, mine's a rum and Coke if you're going past t'bar!

I'll not stop actually, but I did just want to say – bravo Jack! I'm made up you managed to get a crew! You did it! I don't know how but you did it! I mean all them weeks and one letter, one! How much did you spend on adverts? Tell 'em.

JACK *shakes his head.*

(*To* PAUL.) Cos you know he gets his post sent to the office, up at the caravan park, and there I was, I thought, he's spent who knows how much – thousands, wan' it? Thousands. He's got me ringing up *Sailing Today*, *Ships Monthly*, *Yacht World*, what are the others? *Yacht Masters*, *Yachting Weekly*, *Take Yacht and Party*, ha! So imagine me, in me little office cabin, braced to be flooded with letters from all over the globe, giant sacks of mail like at Santa's house and how many replies do we get? One! One!

Laughs.

And! And, and, and, it's from some little old lady in Torquay! Some posh widow in her seventies! I mean we can laugh about it now can't we? Can't we? Can't we?

SUNNY *notices the awkward looks.* JACK *brightens.*

JACK. There's still room for you if you'd like to come aboard Sunny?

SUNNY. And leave the caravan park – peak season?! Don't even joke! Are you hearing this?! Peak season! We're fully –

peak season, Jack. I'd be very popular then wouldn't I? Not! Plus our Jazz is getting married. Ooh! Speaking of.

SUNNY *collects her cocktail, heading off but stops.*

So where did you find them?

JACK. Find who?

SUNNY. Your crew?!

JACK.... I have my ways.

SUNNY. 'I have my ways.' What is he like?! You going Paul? You lived int' North Pole didn't you?

PAUL. Labrador.

PUB BLOKE. 'Labrador'?

PAUL. North-eastern peninsula of Canada. I was a missionary. It's quite fascinating actually because the northern climate is classified as 'polar' but the southernmost parts are 'subarctic' so technically I haven't been to the Arctic.

–

SUNNY. Well. Still be a dab hand. Fighting yetis and that.

PAUL. I'm not going.

SUNNY. No matter now I guess, right. Last chance, smile!

SUNNY *takes another photo.* JACK *half-heartedly smiles.*

A waste of film! Honestly! Safe travels. Smell ya later!

SUNNY *exits.*

PUB BLOKE. Have I got hold of wrong end oft' stick? The one that looks like her off *Golden Girls* said you got an armada, this one says you got one old lady – which is it?

JACK *wrestles with it for a moment. He paints on a smile.*

JACK. You'll just have to keep an eye on the papers!

JACK *pats* PUB BLOKE *on the shoulder, leaving with a jovial smile – but* PAUL's *suspicious...*

PAUL. Jack?

PAUL *follows* JACK *outside. The music and crowd noise dims.* JACK *lights his pipe.* PAUL *joins him.*

Jack... we've been friends a good while now and... long enough, I hope, to know I won't laugh or judge. You don't have a crew?

JACK. No. No, I do. There's three of us. Me. An admiral's widow from Torquay. And Edna. So me and two old ladies. Where's Clegg and Compo ay – I'm a bathtub short of it being *Last of the Summer Wine*! But, if I had two more men for the heavier work... Doesn't matter.

PAUL. So you're not going?

JACK. Let's say no more about it.

JACK *won't meet* PAUL*'s eye. A sad silence.*

PAUL. Well, Gordon'll be pleased, he was moaning you were going to run out on your bar tab!

JACK. Is that supposed to be comforting?!

PAUL. Sorry! You said you don't want to talk about it?

JACK. I don't. Eyes on the horizon! Settle in to another summer here. Chugging round the bay... day trips for the tourists –

JACK *winces as he remembers* –

Oh! Except I can't even do that now!

JACK *hands* PAUL *the detention order from the DOT.* PAUL *reads it.*

Department of Transport. I'm not to leave the harbour due to the life-threatening peril of the ship's bell being too small. Oh – and I don't have enough fire buckets to sail to the Arctic! Have you ever seen anything so mad – I've half a mind to take that detention order all the way to Jan Mayen, pin it to the backside of a polar bear and send them a photograph.

PAUL. So why don't you?

JACK. Are you inciting me to break the law, vicar?

PAUL. Absolutely not. Jack, this list, it's all such small fry! Fire buckets, frayed rope... look I'll come and help you fix all this once the summer holidays are over and that'll give you more time to recruit anyway. Win-win.

JACK. The ice floes'll start to set in if it's left any longer. I've no time, no crew, I'm scuppered.

PAUL. But this was your dream? You've talked of it ever since I've known you.

JACK (*with a shrug*). So it'll stay a dream. Night Paul.

PAUL *watches* JACK *leave*.

PAUL. I should get going too really.

Need to have a chat with Ruth about this trip to the Arctic I'm taking soon. I should dig out a coat shouldn't I? And some woollies.

JACK. Don't be daft.

PAUL. Well I think it'll probably get cold Jack, I know it's summer but it's still the Arctic.

I can bring my old nursing handbook and get together some medical supplies – but I will need to clear it with the bishop.

JACK. It's a long a trip –

PAUL (*counting on his fingers*). Let's see, there was the mission in Labrador, Suriname, Madagascar – narrowly escaped amoebic dysentery from the jungle there. This'll be a bit boring in comparison but I'll give it a go. So, now you only have to find one more man.

JACK. You really want to come?

–

PAUL. Yeah. Why not?

JACK *is overcome, he doesn't know what to say. He sticks his hand out*. PAUL *shakes it*.

Just jump through a few hoops with the DOT Jack. Play nice. Get a bigger bell. Look at the bigger picture! Just get things in order and we can set sail with a clear conscience.

JACK. Thank you Paul.

JACK *moves toward* PAUL. PAUL *opens his arms expecting a hug*. JACK *ducks out the way.*

Get off. I'm shaking a tail feather – if we're going to the Arctic, Gordon can whistle for his bar tab!

JACK *gleefully rushes off.*

Scene Three

The Crew Assembles

Projection: 'A few days later, Whitby Harbour.'

A peaceful summer's evening. PAUL *wanders along the harbour wall where the* Helga Maria *is moored. He takes out a Dictaphone and speaks into it.*

PAUL. So umm, hello, uh me, or whoever ends up listening to this tape. It's ten-past eight on the thirtieth of July 1991. I've had my dinner. We had toad-in-the-hole and a Viennetta, for a last-night treat with Ruth and the girls and now we're just going to do the last bits of loading before, well, heading off to the Arctic in the morning!

I don't know why I said that bit about the Viennetta, just record over that later.

My stomach's a little... not the Viennetta's fault! Just beginning to sink in a bit I think. It's a two-thousand-mile round trip! Two thousand miles!... that's a good old way...

There wasn't time for the bishop to sign off but I did send a letter... it'll be fine I'm sure. What's the worst he could do?! Excommuni– he won't! He wouldn't. No...

Well, let's climb aboard! I'll give you a tour.

PAUL *climbs aboard the* Helga Maria. EDNA *is on deck excitedly and incorrectly peering at the sky with a sextant.* PAT STUBBS *is mopping the deck, wearing an apron and rubber gloves.*

EDNA. Oh it's moved again.

PAT. You must pick one fixed point –

EDNA. But how can you when the sea's all, well it's always in motion as are the stars –

PAT. Yes but generally the horizon does tend to stay level.

EDNA. But when one is upon a boat which is upon the ocean – oh Paul, do come and have a go on Patrica's sextant. It's marvellous!

PAT. It's upside down and it's Pat.

EDNA. Beg pardon?

PAT. My name is 'Pat'.

EDNA. Surely you're a 'Patricia' and it's such a lyrical name, I must say it quite puts 'Edna' to shame. Is it Italian? Patrizzia!

PAT. No. It's Pat. Just Pat.

–

PAUL. Pat, perhaps, do you have a minute now to introduce yourself to the tape?

PAT. Is this the official record of the voyage?

PAUL. As much as anything I suppose.

PAT. Very well.

> PAT *puts down the mop and stretches her hand out;* PAUL *hands over the Dictaphone.* PAT *peers at it, turning it over in her hands.*

PAUL. The record button is –

PAT. Yes, I know.

> PAT *peers at it a little longer.* PAUL *hesitates, a little nervous to offer help.*

> PAT *senses him hovering and puts a finger up to stop him. She takes a cloth and thoroughly wipes the Dictaphone before pressing record.*

My name is Pat Stubbs and I live in Cornwall and I came up to Whitby on Monday and have stayed two nights aboard this ship. It is an unusual ship. I have done a bit of sailing in my lifetime on various vessels including the *Lord Nelson* and sailing a Gypsy on the Mediterranean and now I'm looking very much forward to going to the Arctic. All the stores are in, it's been heavy work getting them in but they're in and stowed, we hope, successfully. And looking forward, very much. To the trip. I'm now signing off.

PAT *hands the Dictaphone back.*

PAUL. Thank you Pat that was thorough.

EDNA *holds out her hand for the Dictaphone.*

Oh we've already got your / bit –

EDNA. I've since had further musings.

PAUL *gives* EDNA *the Dictaphone. She strikes a pose and begins to orate.*

Edna Whelan speaks. Our voyage begins in Whitby and it is with the greatest pleasure I can relate that for me, the magic quality of Whitby has always existed. Here is something magical, rare, thrice-blessed, a holy hill. Where Bram Stoker got his ideas for *Dracula* from I quite fail to see.

PAT *takes a banana from her apron pocket and thrusts it at* PAUL.

PAT. You look green around the gills.

PAUL. I'm fine.

PAT. We can't be doing with seasickness.

PAUL. We're in the harbour.

PAT. Banana, please.

PAUL *accepts the banana.*

EDNA. And though we soon must away to the call of the ocean, looking out upon Whitby's beauty it's as though something pulls your spirit and implores you to stay –

LEWIS (*off*). Could it implore ya to shut up?!

EDNA. Well!

LEWIS TURNBULL *stomps out from below deck, largely cocooned in a sleeping bag, the bottom part unzipped so he can walk.*

LEWIS. We're up at five bleeding a.m. as in the mornin' so let us get some kip, eh?

PAUL *steps forward with an outstretched hand –*

PAUL. We've not had a chance to meet –

LEWIS *grabs* PAUL*'s banana, tossing it overboard.*

PAT. Mr Turnbull –

LEWIS. It's bad luck, d'you not know? You don't have bananas on boats. Or birds, usually. Or vicars. So that's an 'at-trick and we've not left the dock yet. You must be the vicar?

PAUL. And medic. Paul.

LEWIS. Lewis. You done much sailing?

PAUL. I live on a boat, in fact. Just down there.

LEWIS. Oh good man, what type?

PAUL. House.

LEWIS. Comedian eh? What type? Schooner?

PAUL. Canal. Narrowboat I suppose. Never really been sure of the distinction.

LEWIS *looks incredulously up and down the boat.*

PAT. Have you misplaced something?

LEWIS. Just looking for Jeremy Beadle, sweetheart. He's quite a small fella, could be anywhere ya know. Cos someone's definitely taking the Michael here. You know where we're heading?!

But JACK *interrupts, heading briskly down the harbour with a box.*

JACK. Ah good, I see you're all getting acquainted!

PAT. May I ask your position on bananas Captain?

JACK. I didn't take you for the superstitious type Pat?

PAT. I'm not. So if I see any more good, nutritious food being flung overboard I shall have words.

LEWIS. And what words will those be sweetheart?

PAT. 'Don't.' And it's 'Mrs Stubbs' or 'Pat'.

LEWIS *sizes up* PAT. *She is unmoved.*

LEWIS. I think you might be me favourite.

JACK *brings a plaque out from the box.*

JACK. What do you make of this then?

EDNA. Oh it's glorious Jack! Simply perfect! What is it?

PAUL. For the purposes of the tape would you please tell us about this plaque you've unveiled.

JACK *speaks into the Dictaphone.*

JACK. Urr what I have here, in my hands is the plaque that we will soon be erecting on Jan Mayen. The inscription reads 'This plaque was placed here in August 1991 by the crew of the schooner the *Helga Maria* of Whitby to honour the great work in the Arctic of Captain William Scoresby (1760 to 1829). This plaque was donated by Robert Landers meat purveyor of Whitby.'

EDNA. Perfect.

PAT. Very nice.

PAUL. And I will say, a bold advertising move on the part of Robert Landers seeing that it's over a thousand miles from the island of Jan Mayen to that butcher's shop.

LEWIS *laughs, finally, slightly, impressed.*

JACK. Oh yes, I've forgot to read this bit here, it says 'Mention Jan Mayen for a discount on mince'.

They all begin to get the giggles.

EDNA. Free sausages for every polar bear!

PAUL. Ask about our *Helga Maria* meat pies!

An angry looking WIDOW *suddenly shouts at them from the harbourside.*

WIDOW. Shame on you! On all of you. It's just a joke to you isn't it? Isn't it?!

JACK. Can we help you, madam?

WIDOW. And you're the worst of all. 'The great Captain Jack.' You know better, or you ought to if you're half the sailor you make out to be. Look at you. Stood about laughing. And that's how you'll be remembered, fools. The lot of you.

PAUL. I'm sorry, I don't understand –

WIDOW. You're a vicar aren't you? And you got some silly notion to follow this lying chancer out to sea. Well to those of us who's lost folk – and proper sailors at that – my Eddie had thirty years on a trawler and my youngest, Robert. Twenty-six he were. Fit as a butcher's dog, strong, capable and he never came back, neither of them, so what hope have you lot got? What's got into your heads? Have you not got one ounce of sense between you?! Sailing to the North Pole for a jolly?! Shame on you! How dare you play at it. Well I'll not weep over a single one of you. You got no clue. And what's worse, no respect.

The WIDOW *exits, leaving them all dumbfounded, chastened, worried.*

PAUL. That poor woman.

EDNA. Yes, quite, to lose a husband and a son. Colours your whole world something like that.

PAT. I think it's time to turn in.

EDNA. Time for a nightcap more like!

PAT *and* EDNA *go below deck.* LEWIS *shakes his head.*

LEWIS. Vicars, birds and bananas. Well I'm off to smash a few mirrors, moonwalk under a few ladders just for good measure!

PAUL. Perhaps you'll bring us good luck then Lewis, balance things out a bit?

LEWIS. Huh. In case you can't tell, luck's not really me strong point.

LEWIS *goes below deck.*

JACK. So everything's shipshape. You should turn in.

PAUL. That woman just then –

JACK. It's not a 'jolly'!

PAUL*'s not convinced.*

I'm sorry for her but she's wrong Paul. We'll be grand.

PAUL *nods and turns to go.*

PAUL. Best be off, last night at home with the girls.

JACK. Paul – you do trust me?

–

PAUL. Aye Captain.

The sun sets.

Scene Four

Set Sail

Projection: 'Whitby Harbour, 6 a.m....'

'Freedom! '90' by George Michael.

PAUL *arrives with his bags and boards the* Helga Maria *to see his fellow crew buzzing around with final preparations.* LEWIS *hoists a sail.* EDNA *takes photos.* JACK *surveys the weather.* PAT *brings a stack of loo roll aboard.* PAUL *gives* PAT *an apology banana.*

JACK *gathers everyone.*

JACK. So, this is it folks, a few last words –

LEWIS. 'Last words' startin' on a positive.

JACK. It's the cat-o'-nine-tails for insubordination Mr Turnbull!

LEWIS. Aye Cap.

JACK. I'll be straight with you, it's a fair old jaunt to Jan Mayen and once we're past the Outer Hebrides it will be, this, just this, from bow to stern, this will be the whole world. It's likely to be choppy, more than choppy once we're north of Greenland and it'll be hard work. We'll be sleeping in shifts four hours on, four off and the facilities are what they are.

PAT. 'Bucket and chuck it' as we say.

EDNA. You say that in Torquay do you?

JACK. Very apt –

EDNA. Rather crass.

PAT. It's Cawsands actually not Torquay.

JACK. It may not be easy but I can promise you it will be magnificent. The tide is with us, new horizons are within our grasp so this the last chance to disembark before we set sail. Any takers?

The crew look from one to another. EDNA *is resolute,* LEWIS *resigned,* PAT *determined,* PAUL *nervous.*

EDNA. Not I.

PAT. Ready Captain.

PAUL. Let's go.

–

LEWIS. Already unpacked me toothbrush.

JACK. Stand by to make sail.

LEWIS *rings the bell.*

Lewis, cast off the lines.

LEWIS *does so.*

LEWIS. Lines clear.

JACK. Pat, get ready to hoist.

PAT. Ready.

JACK. Hoist.

PAT. Fair winds and following seas.

JACK. Paul, unfurl the Genoa, remember how I showed you?

PAUL. Yes, I mean, aye Captain.

EDNA. And me Jack?

JACK. Wave goodbye to Whitby Edna.

The crew play their parts – there may be other crew reports and commands here, e.g. 'anchor's home' 'bow clear'.

The Helga Maria *sails out of Whitby Harbour.* EDNA *waves enthusiastically.*

EDNA. Oh Jack, isn't it exciting! Isn't it a sight!

JACK. That's the best place for land.

EDNA. What do you mean?

JACK. Out of sight. The best place for land is out of sight.

And they're out, heading into open sea.

Projection: 'Day 1.'

And a route map.

BRENDA *storms across the dock and slams into a phone box. She finds some 10p pieces, angrily feeds them into the machine and dials out.*

BRENDA *(into phone)*. Yes? Hello? It's Captain McCawlee calling from Whitby Harbour. He's bloody done it! They've gone. Take this down. Oh-seven-hundred-hours, thirty-first of July. The *Helga Maria* has relocated from Whitby Harbour in defiance of the detention order served by the DOT. We are henceforth issuing an alert to all naval vessels and the maritime and coastguard agency. Report any and all suspected sightings of the green-striped two-masted sixty-five-foot schooner, named *Helga Maria*. Current location unknown – but we will find them.

We'll find them and when we do we'll throw the bloody book at them!

End of Act One.

ACT TWO

Scene One

Dribbles and Gimbals

At sea! Conditions are choppy but manageable. JACK is at the helm in his wheelhouse. PAUL makes his way unsteadily along the deck with a cup of tea and his Dictaphone.

Projection: 'Day 2.'

PAUL (*into Dictaphone*). So, day two and I am beginning to learn the art or perhaps rather the impossibility of doing even the simplest of tasks on board a boat, namely having a cup of tea and a cigarette. A very delicate operation it turns out, only the most foolish of sailors would attempt the two! I am currently wearing my first cup of tea on my trousers and most of the second on my sleeve. You see if you put your tobacco down, it rolls away but if you put your tea down, it falls over. 'We've had it easy so far' says Jack with the weather – but the struggle to get vertical is quite fantastic.

EDNA staggers on deck looking very nauseous.

Oh hello Edna, feeling any better?

She stands for a moment –

EDNA. Oh dear.

– before rushing back off to be sick.

PAUL (*into Dictaphone*). Edna, poor soul's been seasick from the start really. So she's a bit of a worry to us at the moment. Luckily the rest of us have found our sea legs and we're... beginning to learn the boat. And each other.

The sea gets really choppy, big waves. LEWIS staggers on deck.

LEWIS. Got a light, vicar?

PAUL. If you can get here you can have it. I've got to hold on!

LEWIS *makes his way unsteadily over to* PAUL. *He shouts at the sea.*

LEWIS. Calm down you wet bastards, I'm just tryna get me ciggie lit!

JACK *calls from the wheelhouse.*

JACK. Glorious isn't it!

PAUL *and* LEWIS *head over to the wheelhouse.* LEWIS *is still trying to light his cigarette.*

You see those two blues, where the sea kisses the sky, all of that's my living room. My living room ends where the two blues meet.

PAUL. Lots of room for a sofa.

JACK. Don't you feel it? You can finally breathe out here.

LEWIS (*coughing*). Freedom eh?

JACK. Freedom's a funny thing. I'm free to go nowhere and everywhere. Nowhere and everywhere.

LEWIS *exhales smoke from his now lit cigarette.*

LEWIS. Well I have no idea what that means but I'm all for it. Nothing but sea and sky. No one to nag, no one to interfere.

The bell sounds from the galley below deck.

Almost no one.

JACK. Paul, you take the wheel while I grab some dinner.

PAUL. Me?!

JACK. You can do it. Mr Turnbull here can lend a hand.

PAUL *takes the wheel from* JACK *with a little thrilled/ nervous squeak.* LEWIS *shakes his head.* JACK *exits.*

PAUL. I can't get over how vast it all is.

LEWIS. Vast... and violent, like me mother-in-law eh?!

PAUL. Oh, are you married Lewis?

LEWIS.... nah, just having a crack. Broken heart in every port, me. That's why it's lucky where we're going the only birds are penguins!

PAUL. Penguins are only in the South Pole I'm afraid. It's a common misconception, polar bears and penguins, they're never actually in the same place. Still we'll most likely see some Arctic terns and fulmars. Guillemots and gulls of course, gannets we're all familiar but maybe, just maybe, a shearwater if we're lucky!

–

LEWIS. You know this is a long trip yeah mate? Don't make it any longer than it has to be.

LEWIS *heads downstairs.* PAUL *panics lightly –*

PAUL. Lewis? How do I – I'm not sure where I'm aiming?

LEWIS *(calls).* Just don't move your hands.

PAUL *cranes after him, accidentally turning the wheel as he does. The boat lurches.*

PAUL. Oh dear.

LEWIS *(calls). Don't move your hands!* Stand still and hold the thingy.

PAUL *concentrates fiercely on not moving.*

We follow LEWIS *downstairs to the main saloon just off the galley, where the crew can sit around a table and eat. He helps himself to dinner.*

EDNA *valiantly nurses a box of crackers.*

PAT *holds on to a chemical toilet and appeals to* JACK *as he eats.*

PAT. We need a stronger catch on the head's door which, at current time, is apt to fling itself open without warning. And some sort of stop so one doesn't have to chase down the lavatory and stop it racing into the galley.

PAT *whips out a pad from her pocket which she consults.*

Item Seven. Gimbals. For the cooker.

EDNA. What's a gimbal?

JACK. It's so the hob can rock as the boat does.

EDNA. Ooh I need those, gimbals for me too!

PAT. Gimbals are a necessity I'm afraid Captain. At present the only way to stop everything on the hob from slopping everywhere is to position a secondary pan in hopes of catching whatever tips over. I suggest we get some when we refuel. Item Eight. The tap is half coming off and there's barely enough pressure so the water just about dribbles –

LEWIS. You getting all this Skipper, that's dribbles and gimbals oh my!

JACK. Oh my.

PAT. Item Nine. Algae in the water barrels so we are already running out of fresh water on day two –

JACK. I must go and relieve Paul.

JACK exits.

LEWIS. Ay, leave that there Pat and I can relieve meself!

PAT wheels the toilet out, quietly fuming. LEWIS *sings the shanty 'The Anchor Song'.*

(*Sings.*)
Heh! Walk her round. Heave, ah heave her short again!
Over, snatch her over, there, and hold her on the pawl.
Loose all sail, and brace your yards aback and full –
Ready jib to pay her off and heave short all!

EDNA interrupts applauding.

EDNA. Oh so wonderful! Where did you learn all these marvellous shanties?

LEWIS. Well I cut a little coupon out the back of the paper and they sent us three cassettes and an instructional manual – *on boats* Edna, where d'you think?

PAT returns and makes tea.

EDNA. Have you been sailing all your life? You know Jack went to sea at fourteen. Fourteen! Can you imagine! What about you Lewis? Come to think of it, how old are you? I can't quite pin you down.

LEWIS. Old enough to know better, yet here I am.

(*To* PAT.) I'll have a brew, if you're making one, ta.

EDNA. So how long have you been sailing?

LEWIS. Can I not get a bit of scran in peace?

EDNA. I'm only being personable. Do your family sail?

LEWIS *holds up his mug to* PAT. *She pours tea into it from a teapot.*

LEWIS. Any chance there's whisky in this?

PAT. No. Sugar?

LEWIS. No thanks honey-buns.

EDNA. So you met Jack on the harbour?

LEWIS *nods, taciturn.*

And?

LEWIS. And?

EDNA. Well you arrive in Whitby from you won't say where and meet Jack and the next day you're sailing out to the Arctic! It's all rather mysterious if you don't mind my saying.

LEWIS. I do mind.

EDNA. I didn't mean any offence –

LEWIS. Eat your crackers.

PAT. Since we are all living in such cramped quarters perhaps it would do well to respect each other's space.

EDNA *considers for a moment.*

EDNA. Since we are all living in 'cramped quarters' it's perhaps as well we know who one and other is. I say this without judgement Lewis, Paul will vouch for my Christian character, but are you a vagrant?

LEWIS *stops eating for a moment, keeps his eyes fixed ahead.*

I was advised by a close associate that you were sleeping rough in the harbour. That's how you met Jack?

LEWIS *decides to smile.*

LEWIS. How about this Edna, sweetheart, you don't ask where I've been sleeping and I won't ask you neither.

EDNA. I can't think what that's supposed to mean!

LEWIS. Why are you on this boat eh? Me and her's the only ones any experience –

EDNA. It was the call of adventure Lewis!

LEWIS. Was it?! You'll soon change your tune. You think you're sick now Edna, wait till we get out past Scotland when the going gets really hard. This is easy mode.

EDNA. Oh you don't scare a Yorkshirewoman with talk of things being 'hard'.

LEWIS. An admirable sentiment sweetheart / but we need jobs doing –

PAT. That's 'Mrs Whelan' to you.

LEWIS. This is hard graft, there's work to be done, what are we gonna use you for – ballast?

PAT. Mr Turnbull, Mrs Whelan is a member of this crew and as such is deserving of your respect and civility. Thank you.

LEWIS. I just want her to fess up to why she's really here. That's all.

EDNA. For an adventure. Same as anyone. Adventure called, lured, gripped me in and I could never resist the dark smiling face of adventure.

LEWIS. Jesus wept. 'The dark smiling face of adventure'?! I know what smiling face it was – oh *aye, aye Captain*!

EDNA. I cannot fathom to what you are referring.

LEWIS. How about this, I got another song for ya, Edna darlin'.

LEWIS *pounds a rhythm on the table and sings the shanty 'The Lifeboat Girl'.*

(*Sings.*)
I'm off to see my darlin' Jen,
She's hanging around the slip again.

With her blue eyes, sparkling deep sea-blue eyes.
Giving the crew the old eye-oh,
She wants a lifeboat man!

She heaved herself into the sea, screamin'
'Come on boys won't you rescue me!' /
With your blue eyes –

PAT. Mr Turnbull that's enough! I have had quite enough of
your disrespectful, unprofessional attitude and it is
unconscionable that it should continue. I don't wish to have
words with Captain so I trust you will deport yourself in
a more respectful manner henceforth.

LEWIS. You're dead sexy when you're angry Pat.

PAT. And you are boorish, sexist, tedious and / rude.

LEWIS. It's called 'desire' just give in to it –

PAT. Out! Get out of my galley this instant.

LEWIS *heads out, grinning and singing.*

LEWIS (*sings*).
Giving the crew the old eye-oh,
She wants a lifeboat man!

Radio static.

Scene Two

McCawlee on the Air

RADIO HOST (*voice-over*). And with more detail on the story that is gripping the nation, we have Captain Brenda McCawlee.

BRENDA *steps up to a microphone wearing headphones.*

Thank you for joining us here in the studio. The story of a rogue sea captain who's set off in a condemned ship with his mate the vicar, it's quite extraordinary! The *Daily Express* has 'Skipper Waives the Rules and Heads for the Arctic' arf arf! The headline of the *Mirror*: 'Sail-away Captain and Vicar Head for a Storm. All shipping on high alert for Captain Birdseye lookalike.' Help us sort fact from fiction, is this true?!

BRENDA. Sadly for all involved yes, I can confirm that the Department of Transport has put out an alert to all naval and commercial shipping vessels to find Jack Lammiman and his crew. We believe they are undertaking an illegal voyage to the Arctic Circle and, as such, the *Helga Maria* has been put on a watch list which makes it liable to detention in the ports of fourteen countries. Now we are gravely concerned about the safety of all those onboard. The *Helga Maria* failed a number of crucial safety checks and Arctic waters are fraught with hazards; sub-zero temperatures, storms, visibility issues, ice floes, killer whales, polar bears, the list goes on.

RADIO HOST (*voice-over*). So you're saying the papers may be having a bit of fun but this is no joke?

BRENDA. Absolutely, *we're talking life and death.* We are currently unsure who's aboard but for trained mariners this is a difficult journey; for an untrained crew sailing into these waters this is foolhardy verging on suicidal. So we are appealing for anyone, any shipping, commercial, leisure craft, anyone in a port – if you see the *Helga Maria* please report it. We just hope we find them before it's too late.

Scene Three

Foula Play

Aboard the Helga Maria, LEWIS *and* PAUL *hoist a sail and are startled to see* EDNA, *in a chair, tied to the mast quite happily.*

EDNA. Marvellous morning shipmates!

LEWIS. Jesus!

PAUL *and* LEWIS *stare at her.* PAUL *rubs his eyes.*

PAUL. Can you see Edna tied to the mast?

LEWIS. Unfortunately yes.

PAUL. Thank goodness, I didn't know if I was starting to see things. I don't think I've slept. It's hard not to roll out the bunk and then this 'four hours on, four off'...

PAUL *yawns, clearly exhausted.*

EDNA. Yes, I was having a little trouble keeping upright so Jack tied me up. The fresh air is a real tonic.

PAUL. I'm not sure this is entirely safe?

EDNA. It was Jack's idea and I have total faith in him.

PAUL. I think we should maybe get you back in your bunk.

PAUL *unties* EDNA.

LEWIS. Or lash you to the bowsprit, like a figurehead eh?

EDNA. Ooh that does sound fun!

LEWIS. Least that way you'd be doing a job.

A sour moment.

JACK *appears and rings the bell.*

JACK. Land ho!

Projection: 'Day 4. The Shetland Isles.'

The Helga Maria *docks on Foula in the Shetland Isles, a vast grassy wilderness of cliffs peppered with wild flowers and grey cottages. Gulls call, sheep bleat.*

Welcome to Foula. Also known as 'The Edge of the World'.
Last stop to refuel, get supplies.

PAUL. From where? Can't see anything but sheep and cliffs.

They begin to disembark.

LEWIS. Dear Lord, let there be a pub.

EDNA. Or a hairdresser?

PAUL. Is there a phone box? Be nice to call home. Wonder how
everyone's getting on.

PAT. Bet they've hardly noticed we've gone.

A helicopter buzzes overhead. They watch it.

Scene Four

Sunny Fields the Press

Projection: 'Greendales Caravan Park, Whitby.'

Summer, peak season! SUNNY *is speaking on a landline.*

SUNNY (*into phone*). Jack is a very *very* experienced captain.
Sailed the Seven Seas! Are there Seven Seas? I don't know
how many there are but Jack would've done 'em all. So all
this, 'he's gone off in a tin bath' it's cobblers!

Listens.

Yes you *can* quote me on that. Now is that all cos I got a
queue of campers, a leaky shower block and a nana with
a black eye from a swingball incident.

(*Shouts.*) Not 'black eye', it looks fine! Just keep the ice
pack on, love.

(*Into phone.*) Coming out tomorrow, Tuesday, makes no odds
to me. S'all chip paper int it?!

Listens.

Well not everyone reads *The Times*. Yep, ta-ra.

SUNNY *hangs up.*

Honestly, once swelling's down you'll hardly notice. You did bring sunglasses didn't ya?

The landline rings. SUNNY *answers.*

(*Into phone.*) Greendales Caravan Park, Sunny speaking.

Listens.

Is this *Mail on Sunday, again*? No, I couldn't give a fig if it's a three-part pull-out, I'm trying to run a caravan park here – peak season!

SUNNY *hangs up. The landline immediately rings again, she answers.*

Jesus wep–

(*Into phone.*) Greendales Caravan Park, Sunny speaking.

Listens.

I'll stop you there, are you a camper or a paper?

Listens.

No, for the gazzillionth time *I do not know where Jack Lammiman is*! And I tell ya, if I did, I'd wring his bloody neck!

Scene Five

Frank's Tanked

11 p.m. aboard the Helga Maria, *anchored off the coast of Foula. The conditions are still, we hear the water lapping as the boat bobs gently. A full moon shines brightly above.*

LEWIS *lights a cigarette and fidgets impatiently.* PAUL *yawns.* JACK *peers anxiously out to the horizon. The atmosphere is tense.*

LEWIS. Well that's gone eleven now, is this mate of yours gonna show?

JACK. Sure he won't be much longer.

PAUL. Is it usual to have a supply run so late?

LEWIS. No.

PAUL. Why not do it in the morning?

LEWIS. The one night we're anchored up and not on dog watch, we could be having a proper kip –

The sound of a splash. They rush to where they heard the sound. LEWIS *shines a torch.*

PAUL. Just a porpoise or something.

JACK. Seal.

LEWIS. Coulda been a seal, yeah.

JACK. Switch that off. Should preserve our batteries.

LEWIS *switches the torch off. They wait.*

PAUL. Do you think we'll have time to get to the payphone before we set off tomorrow?

JACK. I don't know Paul.

PAUL. Just got the answerphone when I rang home earlier.

LEWIS. I'm sure the missus'll be made up you wake her at five a.m.

PAUL. I think she'd just be pleased to hear from me.

The sound of drunk singing wafts on the wind from the waves below and the loud buzz of an outboard motor as a dinghy draws alongside the Helga Maria. *Inside the dinghy is* FRANK, *Scottish, drunk and tuneless. He sings 'Do Ya Think I'm Sexy' by Rod Stewart.*

LEWIS. Oh Jack you never told us we was meeting Rod frigging Stewart.

JACK. Did you manage to get it all Frank?

FRANK. Oh aye, oil, gas, paint, veg, whisky! But first things first, most important Jack – can I have your autograph?!

JACK. Alright cut the comedy and let's get moving.

FRANK. The famous devil of the high seas! Captain Jack Lammiman the outlaw! I put you a paper in with the rum. Great photos of you Jack!

FRANK struggles to stand, still singing to himself.

PAUL. What's he on about, paper?

LEWIS. Never mind that, he's three sheets to the wind here.

PAUL. Should one of us climb down?

JACK. Let us know when you're ready to start unloading / Frank –

FRANK. Cabbage ahoy!

Suddenly FRANK *hurls a cabbage at the boat; it hits* LEWIS *with a thwack – chaos erupts.*

JACK. Steady Frank!

PAUL. Are you alright Lewis?

LEWIS. No I'm not. He just hit me with a frigging cabbage!

FRANK. And here's another!

JACK. Frank!

FRANK throws a cabbage and then a volley of spuds and carrots. Ad-lib chaos.

FRANK. Carrots!

LEWIS. Oh aye, just warn us if there's a pumpkin coming!

PAUL. Can we just regroup –

LEWIS. Sod this, I'm off to bed.

JACK. Wait, we need the gas canisters. I'm lowering a net
Frank –

JACK, PAUL *and* LEWIS *lower a net over the side of the*
boat as FRANK *wrestles with a large gas canister.*

FRANK. Alright, alright, alright, alright, Big Frank's got ya boys.

JACK. Here's a net if you put the canisters in the net here
Frank –

FRANK. Heads up!

FRANK *hurls the canister at the boat, it hits* LEWIS *in the*
head. Chaos erupts as LEWIS *reels from his head injury.*
PAUL *tends to* LEWIS *and* JACK *tries to ensure the*
supplies get onboard. PAT *appears with a torch.*

PAT. Why are there cabbages rolling about the deck?!

PAUL. Pat over here, we need more light.

PAT. Paul get that potato before it rolls through the scupper.

PAUL. Light Pat, I think Lewis's got a head wound –

LEWIS. Get off us!

FRANK (*to* PAT). Oooh hello young lady.

JACK. Climb down and grab the diesel, it's gone overboard –
the diesel Frank!

LEWIS *bumps into* EDNA.

EDNA. What's happening?

LEWIS. Aw perfect, right on cue. The Queen of Sheba!

PAT. These stores are going to be inedible.

JACK. We need this diesel canister. It's floating away – Frank!

EDNA. Can I do something Jack?

PAUL. Just go downstairs Edna. It's not safe.

JACK. The diesel Frank, it's on your port side –

EDNA. I'm not a china doll you know.

PAT. Oh shut up you silly woman!

FRANK. Got it. Imma bring it to ya!

JACK. No, put it in the net Frank. Paul!

PAUL. Lewis – Jack there's blood pouring from his head.

FRANK. In one –

JACK. Can someone get over here and do something useful?!

PAT. I am retrieving carrots and potatoes that have been / flung –

FRANK. In two –

JACK. Paul!

EDNA. I could help if someone would let me –

FRANK. Three!

> FRANK *hurls himself at the boat with a huge crash and much shouting. Blackout.*

Scene Six

Will They Call It Off in the Shetlands?

Day 5. Dawn. Main deck. JACK *unpacks some paint cans and paintbrushes as* PAUL *reads angrily from the paper.* PAT *nurses a mug of tea.* EDNA *is at* JACK*'s side like a lapdog, 'helping'.*

PAUL (*reads*). 'Britain's answer to Captain Cod has snuck off on an epic voyage to the Arctic Circle in an old tub. All shipping on the high seas is on alert for intrepid sea dog Jack Lammiman and his vicar mate as they make an audacious three-thousand-mile trip in a fifty-year-old condemned fishing boat – '

JACK. We've not got long, I want to catch the tide.

(*Calls.*) Lewis? Come on, look lively.

PAUL. So we're splashed across the national press and what's worse – we're illegal fugitives?

EDNA. What will they say about that in intermediate ceramics! That beats Susan Barnaby and her crackle glaze any day! Does it put my age? Is there a photo?

PAUL *hands* EDNA *the paper, which she eagerly reads.* LEWIS *stomps on deck with a bandaged head.*

JACK. Lewis get a screwdriver.

LEWIS. Is there one in the hold or should I lean over and wait for it to be flung at me head?

JACK. Or there's paintbrushes there.

LEWIS. I'm great thanks for asking.

LEWIS *stomps back below deck.*

PAUL. Jack?

JACK. Paul – are you going to make yourself useful or stand there gawking at that rag?

PAUL. Pat – back me up here? I know I haven't really slept but I'm not dreaming am I? Jack we are fugitives with the navy chasing us and you're blathering on about painting the boat?!

JACK. Yes Paul. Because we're fugitives! We're going to paint black over the green stripes on the hull, remove the bowsprit, that'll change the profile and we'll change the name plates.

PAUL *and* PAT *share a look.*

EDNA. I thought it was bad luck to change the name of a boat?

PAT. Oh wouldn't it be terrible if we had some bad luck?

LEWIS *enters with his rucksack. He hands* JACK *a screwdriver.*

LEWIS. Screwdriver. Screw this. Sayonara. I'm packing up.

LEWIS *searches for his things, packing his rucksack.*

PAT. You're going?

LEWIS. There's a ferry to the mainland.

JACK. I haven't given permission to disembark shipmate.

LEWIS. That's a good one. So your rules count but the navy can whistle?

PAT. Lewis –

LEWIS. Pat, I know you're secretly in love with us and now the boat's losing its only bona fide hunk but this ship of fools is the absolute last thing I need.

JACK. I will ask you once and once only to reconsider.

LEWIS (*pretends to consider*). Errrrmmmmmm? No.

EDNA. Let him go, we don't need him!

PAT. We do actually. We can't sail without him. Lewis please –

LEWIS. Pat, love, I don't need grief, I don't need the *navy coming after us*, I certainly don't need me name in the papers –

EDNA. Your name isn't in the paper! And neither is mine, actually, which is rather an omission.

LEWIS *finishes packing;* PAT *snatches his bag during –*

PAT. Lewis! Please! Paul, can you – Lewis!

LEWIS. Just go home! You're a smart woman Pat so do yourself a favour and go home to your nice house.

PAT. I can't go home! How could I bear it? I was the laughing stock of Cawsands before I was in the paper – can you imagine…?!

'Ooh what do you want to go to the Arctic for at your age?' 'Who does she think she is?' 'I'm going to be part of a historic voyage' I told them. 'I'm doing something rather grand, actually, finally.' *Finally* doing something of note. Gosh. They'd just love for me to come home, tail between my legs.

You're very much needed here Lewis. Your crew needs you. Please.

LEWIS. And what if the bleeding navy catches us?

JACK. Let's get something clear – I am the captain so anything that befalls us, if it does, falls on my head alone. Or are we going to let them stop us? Petty bureaucrats and pen pushers – Paul – you saw that list, you said it yourself it was nonsense. We can't sail cos the bell's two millimetres too small? And because of that we toss away the adventure of a lifetime?! Our chance to do something – you said it Pat – our chance to do

something great? We let ourselves be cowed and shrug and
say 'oh well' and go home to watch telly?! No. Not while
there's breath left in me.

EDNA. Hear, hear!

JACK. Is that the man you are Lewis? Scared? That's not the
man I know. Nor you Paul.

PAUL. But this is, it's, it's – this, changing the boat like this
with the navy after us – it's some sort of skulduggery. We're
on the verge of an international incident now – it's quite
incredible!

JACK. And should anything happen, I as the captain bear sole
responsibility.

PAUL. Then as your friend shouldn't I try to stop you?

JACK. As my friend didn't you compel me to go when I was
about to give up? If you don't want to paint the hull black
Paul then just paint the white bits white. There. You won't
have put a foot wrong.

JACK holds out the paintbrush. Eventually, PAUL *takes it.*

Lewis? Back in Whitby, you asked me for a chance, I gave it
you son.

LEWIS *shifts, considering it. Finally, he drops his rucksack
from his shoulder.*

Is it settled then? Are we committed as one?

LEWIS. We ought to be committed.

Various 'Aye Captain's, 'Yes's.

JACK. I said are we going to the Arctic? say 'Aye Captain'.

Lacklustre 'Aye Captain's.

Stand tall. Heads up. Shoulders back. I'll ask you again, are
we going to the Arctic?

One loud, declarative 'Aye Captain!'

That's more like it shipmates!

End of Act Two.

ACT THREE

Scene One

New Ranks

'Unfinished Symphony' by Massive Attack.

The Helga Maria *sets sail. The wind and swell grow as they head into open water. Helicopters buzz them.*

PAUL *talks into his Dictaphone.*

PAUL. Sunday fourth of August. Heading westerly from the Shetlands before we head north, an evasive course of action due to the helicopters out looking for us. The roll and the pitch of the boat is quite amazing. She ploughs through but every time we hit a wave it almost comes to a standstill –

They hit a wave, suspension for a moment, before dropping to the other side.

Slow going but on we forge. Can't help think what they're all making of this back home.

A PARISHIONER *takes to the pulpit back in* PAUL*'s church in Esk Valley.*

PARISHIONER. Heavenly Father we pray for the safe return of our beloved brother Paul. Please watch over him and all the crew of the *Helga Maria.* And bring them back home to us, safely.

JACK *enters the galley and stops short;* LEWIS *is cooking whilst* PAT *pores over a navigational chart.*

JACK. What's all this?

LEWIS. We been discussing things. We're wasting Pat being in the galley all the time –

JACK. Who's been discussing –

PAT. It was Paul's idea actually. We can split the cooking duties between, well all of us and –

LEWIS. Look I can't navigate me way to the other side of the table. She should be boatswain.

PAT. It does seem a more prudent deployment of resources Captain?

JACK (*smiles*). Hmm.

JACK *leaves*.

PAT. Thank you.

LEWIS. Nah, just makes sense. Age before beauty Patricia.

PAT. More like pearls before swine.

LEWIS *laughs. The map traces a route north. Focus on* EDNA.

EDNA (*into Dictaphone*). This is Edna Whelan, finally finding my sea legs! A great relief, to us all, although the constant vomiting is very slimming! Well, it's all an adventure, so much unknown still... something's bothering Jack. I don't know if it's this business with the navy or the papers, I so wish he'd open up and tell me things. He's an enigma! That's our Jack. A rather wonderful enigma. I know I'd follow that man to the ends of the earth. We all would. There's something in the air though, static perhaps. That kind of heavy, tingly air.

JACK *argues with* PAUL *in the wheelhouse*.

PAUL. It makes more sense to free Pat from the galley –

JACK (*quietly stern*). I should have stamped this out the first time.

PAUL. What first time?

JACK. On Foula. You questioned me in front of the crew and suddenly everyone's got a bloody opinion on how things should run. It's dangerous.

PAUL. I didn't mean –

JACK. I can't abide it Paul. I won't.

Below deck, EDNA *apprehends* LEWIS *coming out of* PAT*'s room.*

EDNA. It's a simple question – what were you doing sneaking out the ladies' cabin?

LEWIS. Me and Pat's having a torrid affair. What's the matter – you jealous? You want some too Edna sweetheart?

EDNA. You may think I'm daft as ninepence but I've seen my share of shifty, lying little boys and you are hiding something.

Back in the wheelhouse:

JACK. You may be used to standing, preaching in your pulpit but you are on my ship now. I am your captain and my word here is law. Because if it's not, if every time I give an order it's up for bloody debate we'll be sunk. If there is no discipline there is no safety, do you understand shipmate?

PAUL. Yes.

JACK. Do you?!

PAUL. Yes Jack.

JACK. 'Yes Captain.'

Below deck:

LEWIS. You know I've seen my share of people like you an' all love. What could possibly make you think I'm up to something? What – you think I'm thieving from the cabins? Why's that eh? Is it me accent, or me skin tone? Or a little bit of both eh?

EDNA. I am not a…

LEWIS. Not a what? A bigot? Then why are you keeping a special little eye on me eh?

EDNA. You're just very…

LEWIS. 'Very'?!

EDNA. Secretive.

LEWIS (*disbelieving*). Is that it?

I've give Pat a lend of me book cos I finished it and she asked. Go on, it's on the bunk, go and check, don't take my word for it will ya?

LEWIS *pushes past* EDNA. *In the wheelhouse:*

JACK. You said you trust me.

PAUL. I do.

JACK. Then you'll follow my orders. Without question. Without hesitation.

PAUL *realises that's not a question.*

PAUL. Aye Captain.

The wind howls and the sea roars. Thunder and lightning.

Scene Two

Faroe Mayhem

Projection: 'Day 11. Off the coast of the Faroe Islands.'

LEWIS *lurches across the rolling deck, whipped by spray, the sky a violent seething purple.*

LEWIS *grabs a rope and sings into the wind. He's drunk and singing 'It Must Have Been Love' by Roxette.*

LEWIS *begins to climb, unsteadily, up into the darkness, up toward the crow's nest. He continues to sing.*

LEWIS *slips! Almost falls. The boat lurches through the waves.* LEWIS *recovers and carries on his mad climb, still singing.*

JACK *rushes onto the deck and rings the bell urgently.* LEWIS *disappears from view.*

JACK. All hands on deck! All hands. There's a gale coming in. Who's at the wheel?

EDNA, PAUL *and* PAT *rush on.*

PAT. Lewis should be on watch. Lewis?

JACK. Drop the main sail and bring in the gib or we'll lose the pair. Edna – down to the bilge, check the pumps. Do it manually if you have to.

JACK takes the wheel. EDNA heads to the bilge. The ropes and sails whip around in the wind; PAT and PAUL race to get the sails back under control.

PAT. Where is Lewis? He should have been at the helm?

PAUL. Could he have gone overboard? Lewis!

PAT. Lewis! Oh God!

PAUL lurches unsteadily, slipping against the railing.

Paul – careful!

PAUL. Every time I think I have a handle on things.

PAT. Tie this off. We need to locate Lewis. Lewis? Lewis?!

PAT uses a torch and peers into the waves. She makes her way toward JACK in the wheelhouse, carefully clipping herself to the gunwale with a carabina.

Captain, we can't find Lewis. We'll never see him in this – permission to use a flare?

JACK. Use a torch.

PAT. I tried with a torch. If he's gone overboard, every second counts.

–

I know you're trying to be invisible but for heaven's / sake –

JACK (*aggrieved*). Fine. Use a flare. Quick about it.

JACK steers, PAUL tries to hold the ropes steady and look over the gunwales as PAT finds a distress flare.

PAUL (*calls*). Lewis? Lewis?

LEWIS *sings, somewhere high above them.*

The wind howls, waves smash the boat. PAUL *peers into the darkness, straining to see or hear;* LEWIS's *voice is just audible through the din.*

Lewis?! Where are you? Pat? Can you hear that?

PAT *makes her way back toward* PAUL *and readies the rocket flare.*

PAT. We'll get about forty seconds of light. Ready?

PAT *aims, pulls the trigger. Nothing. She tries again and again.*

It's not working, it won't fire!

PAUL *squints up into the darkness.*

PAUL. There, he's up in the rigging! Lewis!

Suddenly LEWIS *falls from the sky, tumbling down to the deck with a crash with a yell.* PAUL *loses his footing, smashing his chest into a railing as he falls to the deck with a cry of pain. The sea roars.*

'It Must Have been Love' by Roxette.

Scene Three

Dawn Bleeds

The storm has passed. Dawn begins to bleed across the water. LEWIS *stares out to sea wrapped in a blanket, he's still drunk.* PAT *enters with the flare gun. She gives* LEWIS *an icy look.*

LEWIS (*indicates the flare gun*). Oooh finally, someone's come to put me out me misery!

PAT. Do you know how to fix a flare gun?

LEWIS. Do you know what day it is today?

PAT. It's jammed.

LEWIS. It's my wedding day! Yay!

PAT *ignores him and goes to stow the flare gun back in its place.*

Is that it?

PAT. I don't care.

LEWIS. God you are ice-cold Pat. Ice queen –

PAT. Would you stop trying to get a rise out of me it is very wearying.

LEWIS. I just told you it's me wedding day and / you're acting like –

PAT. Oh bully for you! Is that what you want? Or is it 'poor you Lewis'? 'Poor little baby boy'– you do realise I'm not your mother?

LEWIS. Thank Christ for that!

PAT. In fact, as boatswain I'm actually your superior / officer.

LEWIS. Oh calm down / darlin' –

PAT (*snaps*). 'Oh calm down darlin''! Hey 'love'. Hey 'sweetheart', 'I know you're secretly in love with us!' You endangered everyone on this boat and now… you sit there with the nerve to be pathetic.

–

LEWIS. 'Pathetic.' That's hit the nail on the head there, boatswain, sir.

PAT *regrets that, allows her anger to pass; she'll be pragmatic.*

PAT. It's almost dawn, let's all of us have a fresh start today.

I don't know if the cartridge has leaked, or, this has completely seized. Here.

PAT *hands* LEWIS *the flare gun. He tries to open it.*

LEWIS. Are there more?

PAT. There are cartridges. They look to be about the same vintage. No other flares.

LEWIS. Shit.

PAT. What other nasty little surprises does this ship have in store for us, I wonder.

–

LEWIS. Pat – you don't hate me do you?

PAT. No.

LEWIS. Edna hates us.

PAT. No she doesn't.

LEWIS. I wouldn't mind that but I don't want you to hate me and all. We're pals aren't we? We could be? Mates?

PAT (*wry*). I don't know Lewis. You do gripe on like an old woman.

LEWIS *smiles*.

Scene Four

Entering the Deadzone

The crackle of a radio news report.

RADIO (*voice-over*). An international search has so far revealed no trace of a Whitby skipper and his motley crew, including the local vicar for Egton and Grosmont who set out on an Arctic voyage in a seventy-year-old vessel declared 'unsafe' by the Department of Transport.

Coastguards and port authorities have tried without success to radio the boat which was last seen heading toward the Shetlands –

Radio static. PAUL *is in the wheelhouse trying to make a call over the radio.*

PAUL. This is Paul Burkitt. Trying to get a message to Ruth Burkitt of Whitby, we're all safe and well. I miss you and I'm sorry about the papers but we're –

The radio hisses and crackles.

Hello? Can you hear me? Over?

PAUL *fiddles with the radio, static, nothing. The radar begins bleeping, malfunctioning.*

Jack? You need to come and look at this!

PAUL *races below deck.*

Projection: 'Day 13.'

The route map appears but flashes, glitching, malfunctioning. The whole projection flickers then goes to white static.

A crew meeting in the saloon.

JACK. It's what's known as a 'dead zone'. There's no radio signal, the navigation equipment won't work – for now.

PAUL. Why?

JACK. Magnetic anomalies combined with the atmospheric pressures. It can scramble the radio frequencies and, this morning, it has.

EDNA. Like the Bermuda Triangle?

LEWIS. Let's hope not eh?

PAUL. What does that mean? Is it bad?

PAT. It's not entirely unexpected, just unfortunate.

JACK. In practical terms, it means we were going to stop at Iceland to refuel but instead we'll keep heading north until we can pick up a signal again.

PAUL. Have we got enough supplies to miss a refuelling stop?

PAT. Stores are dwindling but there are fishing rods so if we can catch something, nice bit of cod. We shall have to ration the fresh water.

PAUL. And fuel?

LEWIS (*shrugs*). As long as we don't get lost.

PAUL. But we haven't got any nav equipment to stop us getting lost?

JACK. We won't get lost. Back to it then.

JACK leaves, seemingly unperturbed.

PAUL. How do we not get lost? Visibility's terrible, we're surrounded by water, no landmarks, I haven't seen another boat for days.

LEWIS. It's called 'dead reckoning' you join the dots on the map.

PAUL. That's it? Pat could you navigate –

PAT. I'll do my best to keep track but when the conditions are misty there's no way to navigate by the stars or the sun. And with the Arctic summer there are hardly stars to begin with.

PAUL. Are you all fine with this?

EDNA. Jack wouldn't steer us wrong.

PAT. He is the captain and he's determined this to be our best course of action. We're in it now.

PAUL. I just, is this – what can we do?

LEWIS. Get on with it. We're already in the deadzone, sometimes the only way out is through. Come on vicar, I thought you were supposed t'be the one with faith?

LEWIS gets up and leaves. PAT exits fretfully to the galley. EDNA rubs PAUL's back.

EDNA. Rest up Paul, get some sleep, you're looking ever so peaky.

PAUL. Huh, I couldn't sleep before and now…

PAUL races up to the main deck, holding his rib, wincing at every step. Main deck is misty.

Jack? I'm just trying to get my head round this – as of now, no one knows where we are?

JACK. *I* know.

PAUL. But no one else knows, if we needed rescuing – we painted the boat, changed the profile, we've been dodging the navy, maintaining radio silence.

We haven't seen another ship since we left the Faroe Isles and now we're forging ahead without stopping for supplies. Agh!

JACK. You said you didn't need a doctor.

PAUL. I don't. But would it matter if I did? Is this, this not-stopping is that really to get us out of this deadzone or is it so you can race to Jan Mayen without getting caught?

JACK. This is my boat –

PAUL. It may be your boat but it's our lives Jack.

JACK. You're on watch in two hours. Get some sleep Paul. It's affecting your judgement.

JACK *exits*. PAUL *takes out his Dictaphone*.

PAUL (*into Dictaphone*). This is Paul Burkitt. It's day thirteen, we are… somewhere in the Arctic Circle. Somewhere in a deadzone. Jack says he knows where we are. He's the only one. Supplies are running low and we're not stopping to refuel.

The galley goes dark.

We've no nav equipment to tell us where we are.

The wheelhouse goes dark.

And no radio to call for help.

PAUL *is left in a single shaft of light.*

We're sailing straight into a vast great grey nothingness. Let's hope we make it to –

Snap blackout.

Interval.

ACT FOUR

Scene One

Voyage Through the Deadzone

A dank, ominous mist hangs over the Helga Maria *as she drifts. The sea and sky are all shades of grey, the horizon almost impossible to discern. It's like the boat is lost in time, suspended between worlds.*

Through the mist we hear LEWIS *slowly singing the 'The Anchor Song'.* EDNA *is learning the song, he leaves space for her to repeat the line he's just sung.*

LEWIS/EDNA (*sing*).
Heh. Walk her round. Heave, ah heave her short again.
Over, snatch her over, there, and hold her on the pawl.
Loose all sail, and brace your yards aback and full –
Ready jib to pay her off and heave short all.

Projection: 'Day 16. Somewhere in Arctic waters. Four days since last radio contact.'

PAUL *enters with* PAT, *carrying mugs.*

PAUL. Cocktail hour.

LEWIS. Aww don't tease us.

PAT. Here.

EDNA. What's this latest concoction?

PAUL. Probably best off just drinking it.

LEWIS. Urr there's bits in it.

PAT. Come on, down the hatch. After three, ready? One, two, three.

They toast, drink and wince.

EDNA. That's got a kick.

LEWIS. What is it?

PAT. Hot-water rinsings from the ketchup bottle with black pepper.

EDNA. Well that's all very well but I believe I requested a cappuccino.

PAT. I do apologise madam, I shall have a word with management.

Waves lap gently at the boat.

EDNA. Right. I am determined to see something. Today is the day.

EDNA *covers her eyes then opens her eyes. Nothing.*

PAUL. I see Jack's in his wheelhouse?

EDNA. Where else?

PAUL *nods to the extra mug.*

PAUL. I'll take him this.

PAUL *heads to the wheelhouse.* LEWIS *sticks up his middle finger.*

LEWIS. Can you take him this 'n' all?

EDNA. Lewis.   PAT. Lewis.

LEWIS. Oh in stereo! That's magic.

EDNA. Right, let's have a game.

LEWIS. Ooh let's.

PAT. Good idea.

EDNA. I Spy.

LEWIS. Oh how marvellous Mrs Whelan, may I have the pleasure, nay the honour of going first?

PAT. Sarcasm is the lowest form of wit.

LEWIS. *Is it?* Ahem. I spy with my little eye, something beginning with Please God Kill Me Now.

–

EDNA. I spy with my little eye...

In the wheelhouse, JACK *knocks back the drink and hands* PAUL *the mug.*

PAUL. Tried fishing. Did some occupational therapy. Swabbed the decks for occupational therapy. No fish. At least the decks are clean.

JACK. I saw a petrel. About an hour ago.

PAUL. Did you?

JACK. It's a good sign.

PAUL. I'll take it. What a relief to see anything that's not this relentless grey. I can't even really tell what's up and what's down. What's sea, what's sky, what day it is, where I end and the mist begins...!

JACK. Paul, will you pray with me?

PAUL. Of course. Heavenly Father, we pray that you will watch over us and guide us.

A banging noise rumbles from below deck and something eerie on the wind – singing?

Lead us out of this darkness and into your light.

Banging intensifies, a strange ethereal singing rises above it – JACK *disappears, everything becomes unmoored and surreal.*

(*Starts to lose his thread, disorientated.*) And... keep us... give us the strength... oh how strange, the mast is... the mast is straight up and down so the horizon... that's the mast, it's straight up and down so that's, the sea must be... are we... are we going in circles? I think we're – Jack? Lewis? No, it's, I'm on watch.

(*Checks the time.*) It's six in the um... doesn't matter. Right so, steer straight Paul. That's the mast, it's straight up and down so the sea has to be here, you can hear it. Can you hear that Jack? Can you hear... I can hear singing. I can hear mermaids singing.

LEWIS *roars from the bowels of the ship.*

Scene Two

Losing Their Heads

Below deck. LEWIS (*offstage*) *rhythmically kicks a door.* PAT *stands with her back against it.*

PAT. Stop it! Stop it at once and get a hold of yourself.

LEWIS (*off*). Let me out!

EDNA *rushes in from her cabin where she's been sleeping.*

EDNA. What on earth is going on?

PAT. I've locked him in. He stormed into the galley ranting and raving –

LEWIS (*off*). I'm sick of eating fish!

PAT. Oh grow up!

LEWIS (*off*). Cod stew, cod curry, cod and peas, cod and cod, I'm gonna throw meself overboard!

EDNA. All this over fish?

PAT. It's lack of nicotine. He's run of cigarettes –

LEWIS (*off*). Edna, Edna sweetheart, let us out.

EDNA. Are you going to calm down?

LEWIS (*off*). I'm gonna throw meself overboard!

PAUL *enters,* EDNA *clings to him.*

EDNA. Oh Paul, Pat's locked Lewis in because he's ranting and raving and threatening to throw himself overboard.

PAUL *nods as if thinking wisely, but he's spaced.*

PAUL. Best not open the door then.

PAT. Lewis, I need the matches. Can you slide them under the door?

LEWIS (*off*). Open the door and let us off this bastard boat!

EDNA. Please calm down.

PAT. I couldn't give tuppence whether you jump overboard or not but I need my matches first!

EDNA. Pat!

PAT. He's taken the last dry book of matches and I can't get the bloody gas lit for the stove!

PAT begins punctuating her speech with pounding her fist on the door.

And I need to light the stove so I can spend hours attempting to cook a horrible meal out of meagre scraps that no one wants to eat including me!

LEWIS (*off*). You've lost your mind you mad cow – I'm staying put.

PAT. That's bloody rich coming from you!

EDNA. Where's Jack?

PAT. Painting his cabin.

EDNA. He's doing what?!

PAT. He's painting his cabin. Buttercup yellow. Said it needed doing.

EDNA. Now?! So who's at the helm?

PAUL. I am.

They stare incredulous at PAUL, who is very clearly not at the helm.

EDNA (*calls*). Captain? A word?

PAT. There's no talking to him. Or him. Or him. Surrounded by pig-headed men!

EDNA. Hush now, thank you Pat that's enough. Now I don't like to be a bossy-boots but this is how I see things. Lewis? Will you come out nicely and stop your nonsense if Paul gives you a cigarette?

LEWIS (*off*). Yes.

EDNA. Paul would you oblige?

PAUL. Of course.

EDNA. Pat, will you take a breath and deport yourself like a lady if Lewis returns your match book?

PAT. Yes.

EDNA. Then kindly unlock the door whilst I take the wheel. Thank you.

EDNA *pushes past them and up to the main deck.*

Scene Three

Here Be Monsters

Projection: 'Day 17. Five days without signal.'

The crew are assembled in the saloon. All in a sullen mood, apart from JACK *who seems oblivious.* PAT *is poring over a chart, there is a little light.*

JACK. Just a little case of the channels. Not enough sleep, not enough food, everyone gets a little frayed.

LEWIS. Where are we?

JACK. On course.

LEWIS. 'On course.' 'On frigging course' every time, no need for a ship's parrot eh? Where on the map are we?

JACK. This is exactly why it's best to be occupied –

LEWIS. By painting your cabin?! What's next, the khazi?!

JACK. There's always jobs to be done on a ship, you know that Lewis.

LEWIS. Where are we Skipper?

JACK. I expected better from you –

LEWIS. Where are we?

JACK. I thought you were a sailor but clearly, you belong on land where it'll say 'Bridlington' on every corner!

LEWIS. Pat, dear God, you getting anywhere, please? Tell us.

JACK. Now if you've all finished, there's plenty of jobs need doing.

EDNA. Jack, please, we need guidance. We need our captain.

PAT. It doesn't make any sense, by my calculations we were here at oh-six-hundred so at five knots... but –

EDNA. What?

PAT. What's happened to this? Where's the rest of the chart?

PAT*'s torch sputters out. There's a commotion as* EDNA *and* PAT *search for candles.*

LEWIS. I'll get the next chart, where is it? In the wheelhouse?

JACK. That's all we have.

LEWIS. No, don't, let's not be pulling my leg mate, I've only had two hours' sleep. Where's the next chart?

JACK. The chart stops here. That's all we have.

PAT *lights a candle.*

PAT. Are you honestly telling us there isn't another chart?

LEWIS. Jesus wept!

PAUL. What does that mean? What's happening?

PAT. We're off the edge of the chart. With no working nav equipment. We have no clue where we are.

PAUL. And we painted the boat – you painted the boat –

JACK. We'll hold our course –

LEWIS. What course? You gonna tell 'em?

PAUL. They don't know what we look like or where to look –

LEWIS. Never mind the frigging navy, I couldn't find us! Jesus! Are you gonna tell 'em Jack or am I?

JACK. Now is not the time to panic –

LEWIS. When is?!

PAT. It's the engine isn't it?

LEWIS. We're drifting. Down to our last bit o' fuel so we either use it to try and get somewhere, take a punt see if we can pick up a signal – which we've not been able to for days – or we drift about here. Wherever 'here' is. And once the fuel's gone even if there was a signal, there's no power to run the radar, no lights for anyone to see us, not that there's bugger-all about and no radio to make a frigging mayday call.

JACK. The wind'll pick up –

PAUL. Is that the plan? What's the plan Jack?

JACK. The wind'll pick up again.

PAT. And blow us where? And how will we know? We're hundreds of miles from land, we're not near any shipping channels –

PAUL. What's the plan Jack?

PAT. Stores are virtually non-existent. We're down to our last barrel of water.

PAUL. Jack?

–

JACK. Have faith.

EDNA. Lewis, you can come up with something, ration the fuel surely? We can catch fish, we can boil water – there's still some gas in the canister for the stove isn't there?

PAT. A little. These are our last dry matches. There's two more books, both soaked. There's six dry. Six more matches.

EDNA. Someone is sure to pass, and they're looking for us, won't they look near Jan Mayen?

PAT. We're miles from anywhere.

JACK. I know where we are. You can believe me or not.

JACK *exits*. PAT *slams out*. LEWIS *starts laughing*.

EDNA. Please Lewis, we, we have to keep our heads –

LEWIS. Me great big shot at freedom and we're trapped! Not only can we not move we wouldn't know which direction to go in if we did! We are totally and utterly trapped. D'you understand? We're gonna die! We're gonna die, we're gonna die, we're gonna die – uh me chest, I can't catch me breath. I can't...

EDNA *takes charge of* LEWIS.

EDNA. Hey, hey look at me, look at me. Breathe.

EDNA *bangs the table in rhythm.*

(*Sings.*) Hey, walk her round.

You sing it back to me. Come on.

(*Sings.*) Hey, walk her round.

Lewis.

LEWIS (*sings*).
Hey, walk her round.

EDNA (*sings*).
Heave her heave her short again.

LEWIS (*sings*).
Heave her heave her short again.

EDNA *coaxes* LEWIS *to calm down as they sing. Night falls.*

Scene Four

Jack or Johnnie?

Darkness. The sound of waves lapping against the boat, which lists gently from side to side. EDNA *sweeps a lantern across the bow.* PAT *enters and joins her in the gloom.*

PAT. Edna?

EDNA. Here Pat.

PAT. Thought I'd join you, see a bit of night-time for a change. This Arctic summer, too much daylight.

EDNA. Well, it's lovely and gloomy out here.

PAT. A change is as good as a rest. And failing that…

PAT *produces a bottle.*

EDNA. Pardon me, what's this?

PAT. My secret stash. Johnnie Walker. Purely medicinal of course.

EDNA. Of course.

PAT. Care for a tot?

EDNA. If you insist.

PAT. Don't tell the boys. I have the feeling if Lewis found it the bottle would soon be empty. Do you need a glass?

EDNA. Oh I won't stand on ceremony if you don't.

PAT. Down the hatch then.

PAT *takes a swig straight from the bottle.* EDNA *is impressed and follows suit.*

EDNA. Oooh, that'll put hairs on your chest.

PAT. Now there's a man you can count on, Johnnie Walker. Smooth, fiery and he stays where you put him!

EDNA. Pat?! May I have another go on your boyfriend?

PAT. He's all yours. Edna, may I be, very, candid for a moment?

EDNA. I would absolutely love that. Dish!

PAT. I am utterly, and irrevocably, sick of stupid bloody men. Paul needs a nursemaid, Lewis needs a mother, Jack needs… locking up! How have I let myself end up in this mess?! In fact, come to think of it, every mess I think I have ever been in has been due to pig-headed, bullish, boorish, know-it-all and frankly unhygienic men!

EDNA. Ooh don't hold back Pat, tell me what you really think!

PAT. Don't you think?!

EDNA. Well… yes. Yes, me too. I think a great deal of the messes I've ended up in have probably had a man at the bottom of it – only difference is I enjoy it!

–

Just been thinking about my John, what he'd say to all this. Do you think they're watching us? My John and your Raymond?

PAT. Oh what a thought.

EDNA. Peering down at us! I know exactly what John would be saying – well first, when he'd stopped laughing, which would take no small amount of time I'm sure, he'd shake his head and he'd say 'That's our Edna.' That's what he always used to say. Whatever scheme I'd got myself into, painting, amateur dramatics, African drumming, 'That's our Edna!'

PAT. African drumming?

EDNA. Ooh it's ever such fun, if you get the chance.

What about your Raymond, what would he be saying if he's looking down now?

PAT. …Some very choice words I'm sure.

PAT *drains the bottle and hurls it into the ocean.*

EDNA. Patricia! We could have put a message in that.

PAT. An SOS.

PAT *begins to cry.*

EDNA. Oh Pat.

PAT. I'm sorry, sorry.

EDNA. No let it out, better out than in.

PAT. I so wanted this. All my life, I've been so desperate to have an adventure and now I feel such a fool.

EDNA. You a fool?! Never. What about me then? You know what I said in Whitby, when people said 'what you going for?', people saying I shouldn't trust Jack, I'd look 'em in the eye and I'd tell 'em 'I would follow that man to the ends of the earth' and to my credit, I have...

Look, you wanted to do something Pat and you have! It couldn't be more of an adventure – we are daredevils you and I! Look at us. Flying by the seat of our briefs!

I mean it might be scary but this beats intermediate ceramics, I tell you that for nothing. I don't know when I've felt more... alive.

EDNA *puts her arm around* PAT*;* PAT *lets her.*

PAT. We have to make it out of this. We just have to. I keep wondering if I should take charge of the ship. If I should try and wrest control.

EDNA. And what would you do?

PAT.... I really don't know now, that's the trouble.

EDNA. I know what we do. We keep our heads up. We puff out our chests and we endure come what may. Hey, like a figurehead on the prow. Maybe that's why they always have women on the front of ships! Cos that's what they need, strong women, looking forward. Come on, dry your eyes. Stand tall.

PAT *dries her eyes, takes a deep breath and stands upright next to* EDNA.

PAT. Yes, thank you. Exactly.

You're a remarkable woman Edna.

EDNA. You too.

PAT. I know.

You could do a great deal better than Jack Lammiman.

EDNA. It's the eyes. Always been a sucker for blue eyes.

PAT. Like Paul Newman.

EDNA. Oh Paul Newman! Now there's a man. The eyes! The arms! The salad dressing! Ooh he could dress my salad any day.

PAT (*laughs*). Oh God!

Oh God.

What are we going to do Edna?

EDNA. I spy, with my little eye...

PAT *laughs*.

The sun rises. The sound of waves, mingle with games of 'I Spy' and PAUL *and* JACK*'s whispered prayers...*

Scene Five

Jan Mayen!

Projection: 'Day 19. 6 days without signal.'

LEWIS, PAT *and* EDNA *hang around listlessly on the main deck.* JACK *is in his wheelhouse. Visibility is still terrible.*

LEWIS. I spy, with my little eye, something beginning with 's' –

PAT. We shall not allow you to play any more if you're not going to play properly.

LEWIS. It begins with an 's'.

PAT. Everything begins with 's' if you put the prefix 'stupid' in front of it.

LEWIS. Makes it a challenge then doesn't it?

PAT. Your company is challenging enough without / need for –

EDNA. Look look look! Over there, look. Please tell me you can see that. I spy a mountain! Please tell me it's a mountain?!

PAT. It looks like a mountain.

EDNA. Is it land?!

LEWIS. It is, look, see them waves breaking on the shore. There's a shore!

EDNA. Oh! Shall I ring the bell?!

PAT. Land ahoy!

LEWIS. Thank bastard baby Christ!

EDNA rings the bell.

EDNA. Land ahoy! Land ahoy!

Projection: 'Jan Mayen.'

PAUL and JACK rush to join them from the wheelhouse. Ad-lib excitement and hugs. PAUL winces in pain from his cracked rib when hugged. PAT kisses LEWIS on the cheek, which takes them both by surprise.

The mountainous island of Jan Mayen hoves into view. The sound of walkie-talkie static and Norwegian voices over the radio…

PAT peers through binoculars.

PAT. I don't wish to alarm everyone. But…

LEWIS. Are they…?

PAT. Yes, there appear to be rather a lot of soldiers and they have guns pointed right at us.

Shit…

Scene Six

Up a Volcano in the Dark

A rancorous crew meeting in the saloon.

JACK. So it's confirmed, we have made it to Jan Mayen and for that I think we should all be very proud –

PAT. 'Uninhabited' you said.

JACK. The island has no indigenous population –

LEWIS. Oh did you know he's a lawyer and all?

JACK. It would appear that there are currently personnel from the Norwegian Meteorological Institute and Norwegian armed forces, stationed on the south-east coast. So I say, under the cover of darkness we row the dinghy over to the north side of the island taking with us the plaque, the cement and a couple of fishing poles. We begin our ascent of the main summit, Beerenberg –

EDNA. The mountain?

JACK. It's only seven thousand feet.

EDNA. With my hip?

JACK. Someone needs to stay onboard here in any case so that will be Edna –

PAUL. It's not a mountain, it's an active volcano.

JACK. Is it?

PAUL. Said so in that book.

JACK. Well I doubt it'll go off –

PAT. Why would it? We've been so lucky so far.

–

JACK. Anyroad, upon finding a suitably prominent outcrop, Lewis and I shall mix the cement whilst Paul and Pat keep a look out for the Norwegian army and polar bears.

LEWIS. Polar bears?!

JACK. It's just a possibility.

LEWIS. And if we see a polar bear whilst we're up a mountain in the dark?

JACK. Well just, have at it with a fishing pole. Paul knows.

PAUL. Paul does not know.

JACK. Don't be so modest.

PAUL. I'm not being modest, I may have lived near polar bears but I never 'had at' one with a fishing rod.

JACK. I doubt there will be one in any case –

LEWIS. So all we have to do is carry two bags of cement –

PAT. And the water to mix it.

LEWIS. Thank you Pat, and the water to mix it with. Two bags of cement and water and tools, carry those up an ice-covered mountain, in the dark – without any mountaineering equipment – and the only risks are being arrested by the Norwegian army, shot at by the Norwegian army, being mauled by a polar bear or toppling off a mountain?

PAUL. Active volcano.

LEWIS. Oh yes, active volcano, thank you. I don't know what you're all worried about.

PAT. I vote we throw ourselves on the mercy of the Norwegians? All those in favour?

LEWIS. Aye!

EDNA. Aye, sorry Jack.

PAUL. I'm sorry, it's such a stupid plan and I'm so exhausted.

PAT. The 'ayes' have it.

JACK. What are we going to do with the plaque?

LEWIS. Oh I'll tell you what you can do with that plaque!

EDNA. Lewis!   PAT. Lewis!

Scene Seven

Sunny Saves the Day

Greendales Caravan Park, Whitby, filled with the noises of holidaymakers – kids shouting, radios, it's peak season.

A landline phone rings, SUNNY *answers.*

SUNNY (*into phone*). Greendales Caravan Park?

Listens.

No we're fully booked that weekend I'm afraid, bank holiday int it?

Listens.

No it dun't matter if you don't bring the awning love, there isn't a pitch for ya, sorry. Okay bye, bye.

SUNNY *hangs up and cranes to shout at someone.*

Kev? Have you checked that leak in shower block yet? It's a bloody madhouse.

The phone rings again.

(*Into phone.*) Hello, Greendales Caravan Park? Speak up, the line's dead crackly.

Listens.

Jack? Oh thank Christ you're alright Jack! Where are ya?

Listens.

You made it! And how is everyone? You all alright?

Listens.

Oh I bet you're having a right party onboard! You must be thrilled!

Listens.

Oh?

Oh.

With guns?!

And you want me to what?!

Listens.

Listens.

Listens. Makes a note.

You do appreciate it's peak season, Jack. Peak – How much d'you love me?!

Listens.

That's Jan Mayen but with a J right? Leave it with me.

SUNNY *hangs up and searches.*

Kev? You set eyes on Yellow Pages?! Got to find a number for t'Norwegian Embassy!

'(We Want) The Same Thing' by Belinda Carlisle blasts out of the office radio.

Back in the Arctic, the crew of the Helga Maria *fret and wait.*

SUNNY *is working the phones.*

(*Into phone.*) No, they're not off the coast of Norway – it's an island, Jan Mayen?

Listens.

Yeah the army do know as it happens.

Listens.

Jack's not armed! I don't think.

Later –

(*Into phone.*) William Scoresby... you've not heard of – well I hadn't either to be honest, that bit's not important. They really just want to pop over, take a few photos and they do need to borrow some supplies – Just hang on a mo.

(*Covers the phone.*) Toilet block's two turnings on your left love, take a site map, no the other left.

(*Into phone.*) Sorry about that Mister Ambassador, where were we?

Later –

(*Into phone.*) I mean I've not had any formal diplomatic training but I do judge the talent contest here at the park and that does require a lot of diplomacy, I can tell you!

Listens.

(*Flirty.*) Well if I'm ever in Tromsø...!

Listens.

Oh you will? Thank you! Thank you! I mean, uh –

(*Reads from her notes.*) Takk skal du ha! Goodbye. Ta-ra love, bye.

SUNNY *hangs up and pumps the air in triumph.*

Yes! Champion! Leave it to Sunny!

Scene Eight

Off With His Plaque

The Helga Maria *moored off the coast of Jan Mayen. The crew ready to depart on the dinghy, putting on life jackets, etc.* JACK *pulls* PAUL *to one side.*

PAUL. I can't believe it's happening. I can't believe we're about to actually set foot on the mythical Jan Mayen and I'm going to have a hot shower! I know it's a pilgrimage for Scoresby and I don't wish to downplay that but honestly, Jack, right now the hot shower is pipping it to the post for me.

JACK. Good. You need it.

PAUL. I do!

JACK. Enjoy! And please give this to the camp commander with my thanks.

JACK *hands* PAUL *the plaque;* PAUL*'s bewildered.*

PAUL. Jack?

JACK. Someone has to stay with the boat. Go on.

PAUL. You're not coming?

PAT *interjects*.

PAT. Are we ready shipmates?

LEWIS. Come on come on, I need to get lathered up, get me in that shower!

PAT. Yes, the sooner the better.

LEWIS *sings 'He's a Tramp' from* Lady and the Tramp *and cajoles* PAT *to dance with him –*

Get off, you stinky boy!

LEWIS *sweeps* EDNA *into a ballroom hold and dances with her instead.*

LEWIS. Edna doesn't mind, do ya?

EDNA *sings*.

PAUL (*to* JACK). Jack, are you really –

JACK. Enjoy, you've earnt it.

JACK *strides off to the wheelhouse. The others notice him go.*

PAT. What's happening?

PAUL *shrugs.*

Scene Nine

Skål!

The sound of a noisy mess hall. A NORWEGIAN SCIENTIST raises a toast, with the plaque.

NORWEGIAN SCIENTIST. It is, the most extraordinary and I hope no offence to say, most unusual story of an expedition. As Norwegian people we were unaware of the famous British Captain William Scoresby but he must truly have been a hero of great importance that you would risk such a trip to honour his memory. On behalf of the Norwegian government we thank you for this plaque which we shall be proud to display in our research facility here.

Perhaps on the wall there or in the corridor, Jorgon will find an excellent position for this plaque, won't you? Yes. Thank you Pat and Paul and Lewis for your enormously unexpected visit! We toast to your good health and wish you a safe return to your homeland – which you will need to undertake within the next few hours due to the hazardous tides and the ice floes and polar bears and request from our army friends and the embassy. But first a toast! Skål!

Scene Ten

Great Men

JACK *looks over the bow.* EDNA *sidles up to him wearing her fancy hat and brandishing a camera. He startles.*

EDNA. Ta-dah! Well, what do you think? Told you I bought a hat for the occasion.

JACK *forces a polite smile.* EDNA *points the camera.*

Shall I get one with you and Jan Mayen?

JACK. You're alright.

EDNA. Go on, I've been saving the film!

JACK. No.

EDNA. Come on, after all this way! After everything Jack?!
Crack a smile, say 'cheese'!

JACK *won't pose.*

Oh one photo! Jack! At least let's get one of the two of us?

JACK (*pinched, annoyed*). I'll take one of you how about that?

EDNA *hands over the camera and poses.* JACK *snaps
a photo and hands it back.* JACK *briskly takes out some
binoculars and surveys the water toward Jan Mayen.*
EDNA *hovers.*

EDNA. I should think they'll be another hour.

JACK. I hope not with this tide.

–

EDNA. We should have a toast! To celebrate the voyage!

JACK. Shouldn't drink on watch.

EDNA. No, of course!

–

We could toast with tea?

JACK. I'm fine.

–

EDNA. Well, I think we've done jolly well. Pats on the back all
round! I mean, look at me Jack, the most unlikely sailor and
yet, under your sail, flag, well however you say it, I'm tying
bowlines with the best of them! I've blossomed. Like a
flower that's bloomed in the sun.

–

You know I did wonder why you'd have me come at all?

JACK. You asked to come.

EDNA. I did! I did but... Lewis can sail, Paul's a medic, Pat
can sail and navigate and, well, is there anything Pat can't

do?! I've done my best to be helpful and cheerful but I can't help think, if there were some reason, some other reason, if I had a, special role. I should like to be special. To you.

EDNA *searches* JACK *for answer; he studiously avoids looking at her, his irritation growing.*

JACK. Perhaps that cup of tea.

EDNA.... I think I maybe made a bit of goose of myself then. Silly goose. It's all this sea air. I blame the sea air!

JACK (*snaps*). Edna, for the love of God woman, leave me be!

EDNA *is stung like she's been slapped. She puts on a brave face.*

EDNA. I'll make that tea.

EDNA *goes to leave.*

JACK. I didn't mean to snap. I've...

EDNA *hovers, waiting for him to finish.*

I had such plans. Such a vision for this. And it didn't look like this. It didn't look like this at all.

EDNA. It didn't look like me you mean?

JACK. What are you on about woman?! You make no odds to me one way or t'other. This voyage was about [me] – my hero, Scoresby. A great sailor, a great man who never got his due and *I* was gonna be the one... I was meant to be... I was going to lead a flotilla now I can't even put the plaque on the blasted mountain!

...'Captain Cod' they're calling me in the papers.

How can great men who do great things go so unremarked?! It's a disgrace. I don't wish to celebrate any of this. I don't even wish to remember it.

JACK *leaves* EDNA *stunned on the main deck. A storm blows in.*

Scene Eleven

Dinghy Disaster

A storm, mist is fast descending. PAUL, PAT *and* LEWIS *are in a dinghy in the waters off Jan Mayen. We hear the outboard motor of the little dinghy as it struggles against the waves, the ocean roaring as it bounces the dinghy from side to side.*

LEWIS *is at the tiller and* PAUL *is shining a torch ahead.* PAUL *flashes the torch three times. A light blinks back.*

PAUL. There!

PAT. I make that about fifty feet.

LEWIS. It's not the distance, it's this current. We might have to paddle.

PAUL. We're almost there.

LEWIS. Yeah and the current is dragging us away from the *Helga Maria* so can ya paddle, please.

PAUL. It's not far.

LEWIS. I don't know about you but I don't fancy being swept into the Arctic Ocean.

PAUL. I don't know if I can paddle with my rib.

LEWIS. Sod your rib.

PAT. Focus. Here.

   PAT *takes a paddle. A wave knocks the little dinghy, spinning it off course.*

LEWIS. Dammit!

PAUL. I've lost her.

   PAT *tries to paddle, they look for the light.* PAUL *signals again with the torch.*

PAT. There, to starboard.

   The outboard motor splutters and dies. LEWIS *tries to get it to restart.*

LEWIS. Christ! Does nothing we have work?!

PAT. Seventy –

PAUL. We haven't run out of fuel, I refuelled it –

LEWIS. Shut it for a minute will ya.

PAT. That's more like seventy-five feet now. We're being pulled out.

LEWIS *tries to get the motor to work. The storm grows.*
PAUL *joins* PAT *paddling but it causes him severe pain in his rib.*

PAUL. We'll never make it with paddling.

PAT. If we can just stay in one place, without getting pulled further out –

LEWIS. Come on, come on, ya bastard thing!

Another wave.

PAUL. Shall we turn back? Can we get back to the island?

PAT. I can't even see the island.

LEWIS. It's six o' one half a dozen o' the other. Come on you bastard work!

PAT. Mayday! Mayday! Jack! Edna!

PAUL. Jack! Can you hear us! The engine's cut out! Jack!

PAUL *coughs and groans in pain from his rib.*

LEWIS. We're drifting here! Paddle! Put your back into it!

PAT. Lewis, you paddle, I'll try the engine

PAUL *is still coughing and trying to paddle,* LEWIS *takes the paddle from* PAT.

LEWIS. Put your back into it, come on mate!

EDNA*'s voice rings out from the mist. She's aboard the*
Helga Maria *with* JACK.

EDNA. Jack's getting a rope, see if you can get close enough!

JACK. Okay ready! On my count – one, two, three!

A rope is thrown, PAUL *dives to get it,* LEWIS *grabs his coat to stop him going overboard. The little dinghy rocks.*

LEWIS. Careful! You'll capsize us!

PAUL (*coughing*). We've got to do something. I can't keep paddling.

JACK. Again, on three! One, two, three!

A rope is thrown, it lands in the water. They paddle frantically but can't reach it.

PAUL (*coughing, wheezing*). Our Father, who art in heaven, hallowed be thy name –

LEWIS. Come on, we can do this. Pat!

PAT *grabs the paddle from* PAUL *who collapses, wheezing.*

PAT. Throw the rope!

JACK. Come on, on my count.

PAUL *prays,* LEWIS *and* PAT *paddle frantically.*

JACK. One, two, three!

PAUL *lunges and grabs the rope.*

PAUL. I've got it.

LEWIS. Pull us in Jack!

PAUL *secures the rope.* LEWIS *and* PAT *paddle.*

PAT. Finally going in the right direction.

EDNA. We've got you now!

JACK. Keep paddling, we'll reel you in.

LEWIS. Thank Christ eh.

PAUL. Exactly.

Suddenly the rope snaps and they're cast back out by a huge wave.

PAT. No!

EDNA. The rope's snapped!

LEWIS. Frigging rope's snapped!

LEWIS, PAT and PAUL hold on tightly as waves buffet the little dinghy, turning it back around. They're lashed by wind and rain. PAUL and PAT grab the paddles as LEWIS tries the engine again.

PAT. We're drifting back out!

PAUL. I can't even see them.

LEWIS. Come on, you bastard!

JACK. We'll try another rope!

PAT. It's too far.

PAUL. Where are they? I can't see the *Helga Maria*, where are they?

PAT. Jack! Edna! The light!

EDNA. Just hold on!

PAUL (*coughing*). Jack! Jack!

LEWIS. Please, please, please, please.

PAUL. Heavenly Father, please deliver us –

The engine again. It starts! The little dinghy begins to chug in the right direction.

PAT. Oh thank heaven.

LEWIS. Jesus.

Relief.

Scene Twelve

Wounded Animals

The saloon, below deck on the Helga Maria. EDNA *makes tea.*
PAT, LEWIS *and* PAUL *enter, shell-shocked.*

EDNA (*worried*). Tea on the way. Nice and hot, plenty of sugar.

   PAT *is quietly livid; she puts her energy into finding*
   blankets. LEWIS *is emotional, overwhelmed, he supports*
   PAUL *to find a seat as* PAUL *is still wheezing and shaking.*
   PAT *gets* PAUL *a blanket.*

LEWIS (*holding back tears, to* PAT). That was nearly… I mean,
   we could've…

PAT. I know.

LEWIS. I'm going for a ciggie.

   LEWIS *exits.* EDNA *hands out tea.*

PAT. A lie-down I think.

   The storm rages on outside. PAUL *sits stunned, shivering,*
   wrapped in a blanket. JACK *enters with a jumper.* EDNA
   scurries away on seeing JACK. JACK *can barely look at*
   PAUL. *He puts the jumper on the table.*

JACK. Here.

PAUL (*coughs*). I can't get warm.

JACK. You will, soon enough.

   PAUL *tries to put the jumper on but winces from the pain in*
   his rib. JACK *comes to help him into the jumper.*

Getting worse?

PAUL. Just the cold and the exhaustion I think.

   JACK *goes to leave.*

Is that it?

You've not said two words to me after – that. Whatever that
was Jack! Hauled us in and you just left me there, lying on
the deck like a wounded animal.

JACK. What would you have me say?

PAUL. Do you not care?!

JACK. You've had a shock. You'll recover.

PAUL. We could have died Jack! Been swept out to sea, capsized, drowned, frozen, anything. Why didn't the motor work? Was that on the list? The list from the DOT and the rope, the one that snapped – was that on their list too?

JACK. You're all onboard –

PAUL. Just! It's one thing, thinking the rules don't apply to you, the untouchable, the legendary Captain Jack but what about the rest of us? You promised me it would be alright –

JACK. And you are.

PAUL. Ha! Am I?

No thanks to you Jack. Has it been worth it? Got your plaque on Jan Mayen, escaped the navy, another heroic escapade, sticking it to the man.

JACK. This was your idea Paul. Stop pretending you have no part of it. No one dragged you, forced you. You chose this and every man must take responsibility for their own choices, I have borne mine.

PAUL. I thought we were friends.

JACK. On land. Out here, there's just captain and his crew.

You'll be relieved to know we're heading south. We're done here.

'Farewell to Tarwathie' by Judy Collins. JACK goes on the main deck and we hear the shouts as the Helga Maria *sets sail and PAUL shivers, alone.*

Stand by to make sail. Edna – ready the windlass. Pat – cast off starboard bowline. Lewis – stand by to unfurl the gib.

The Helga Maria *turns south.*

End of Act Four.

ACT FIVE

Scene One

The Last Supper?

The crew attend their duties now with a practised precision like a well-oiled machine as they sail south. JACK stays apart from everyone. Distant. Thoughtful.

Projection. 'Day 22. Off the coast of Iceland.'

The galley. PAUL is reading a book. PAT is looking at charts and making notes. EDNA enters from the main deck.

PAT. You know this voyage is the only time in my entire life in which a man – who was not paid to be a chef – has cooked me a meal. No. Can't think of another! Remarkable.

LEWIS *enters with two bowls.*

LEWIS. Right boys and girls, hold on to your hats and prepare to have your minds blown by a dazzling once-in-a-lifetime culinary experience!

PAT. Ooh what is it?

LEWIS. Stew.

EDNA. What kind of stew?

LEWIS. The Lewis Turnbull special.

LEWIS *exits to get the rest of the bowls. The others look from one to another, wary.*

PAUL. Well he certainly seems very excited about it.

EDNA. Just say grace extra hard Paul. We may need the help.

LEWIS *enters and puts the other bowls down.*

LEWIS. Bon appetites!

PAUL. Thank you.

PAT. Yes, this looks...

LEWIS *tucks in, the others are hesitant.*

LEWIS. Tuck in then.

PAUL *clasps his hands together to say grace,* EDNA *and* PAT *join in,* LEWIS *carries on eating.*

PAUL. Heavenly Father, we thank you for –

EDNA. Harder.

PAUL (*louder*). – these thy gifts we are about to receive. Amen.

They eat. It's delicious. Ad-lib appreciative noises.

LEWIS. 'Thank you Lewis.'

EDNA. Lewis, this is delicious!

PAT. Oh this is wonderful.

LEWIS. It's this little thing called 'flavour' Pat.

EDNA. He's right on that score .

PAT. Charming! Oh thank you very much.

LEWIS. Ooh go on, have a fight! Dinner and a show eh Paul? Was so much more fun when you twos was at each other's throats.

EDNA. We were never / 'at each other's throats'!

PAT. I have no recollection of anything of the sort!

LEWIS (*imitating* PAT). Oh Edna, you must learn to tie a bowline –

(*Imitating* EDNA.) I don't know how they do things in Torquay but it's not the sort of society I would keep. Now let me bang on about my evening classes –

(*Imitating* PAT.) Oh do find yourself some useful occupation, you silly woman!

EDNA *and* PAT *look at each other, incredulous.*

PAT (*imitating* LEWIS). Ay sweetheart, give us a ciggie or I'll have a tantrum like a proper baby!

LEWIS. That's an addiction, it's not funny –

EDNA (*imitating* LEWIS). I'm Lewis and I'm the big I am!

PAT (*imitating* LEWIS). I'm fighting and arguing with everyone cos I'm so manly and virile!

EDNA. Stomp stomp stomp, get us a brew sweetheart stomp!

PAT (*imitating* LEWIS). I'm gonna throw meself / overboard!

EDNA (*imitating* LEWIS). Overboard!

LEWIS. That's nothing like me, so I don't know where youse got that from. Well this is nice eh? 'Thank you Lewis for cooking us a slap-up meal.' Thank Christ it's me last one you shower o' bastards.

PAT. Pardon?

PAUL. You're leaving?

LEWIS. Look I know. You think you'll fall apart with me and Pat's secretly in love with us but you'll be sound. Get someone to check the engine over in Iceland, you'll have supplies, it's only gonna get easier – well, unless the navy gives you a lift eh?

EDNA. Is that why you're leaving?

LEWIS. …just time to go.

LEWIS *carries on eating, the others pick at their food, upset.*

EDNA. No. No, that's not going to happen.

PAUL. None of us want you to leave.

EDNA. We're a crew. We belong together.

LEWIS. Not for much longer. We all gonna carry on doing this are we? Living together, playing Happy frigging Families?

PAUL. What are you going to do in Iceland?

LEWIS. Dunno yet.

PAT. Keep running away. That's what you'll do.

LEWIS *gets up from the table.*

LEWIS. Oh I don't need this.

PAT. Yes you do, you need to hear this. Sit down.

LEWIS. Is that an order, Admiral Stubbs?

PAT. No.

Look, I don't know what we are. What any of us are to each other but I do know we've spent the last three weeks working and living cheek by jowl and very nearly dying together! So I do think that entitles us to show concern. You don't know anyone in Iceland –

LEWIS. I didn't know no one in Whitby neither.

PAUL (*teasing*). Yes and look where that got you.

–

LEWIS. There's nothing in England for me. Nothing but a load of very ticked-off people.

EDNA. And us.

LEWIS (*sarcastic*). Yay!

I feel sorry for you lot actually cos you're all going back to a – and I'll use language you'll approve of here Pat – a total bunfight. A mess, that's what's waiting for each of us, not just me. It's been in the papers – eh you was worried people were laughing at you in Cornwall Pat well wait till you arrive home and you're on the front page –

PAUL. We don't know we're on the front page, it might have blown over.

EDNA. It'll be all over Whitby at least, the gossip in that place.

LEWIS. – eh and never mind the papers what about the government?! They sent helicopters out looking for us you think they're gonna be happy with a slap on the wrists? Naughty naughty. You're gonna stick your neck out are ya and for him?! Would he stick his neck out for us?

PAUL. I mean, you're right.

LEWIS. Thank you.

PAUL. I don't know about Jack, Lewis. I think you could spend a lifetime trying to work out what's going on in the mind of Jack Lammiman. He's the most skilled and knowledgeable sailor I've ever seen and at the same time he's reckless. He spends hours contemplating things deeply and then acts like he's never thought a thing through in his life. And what are we Pat? We're just a hotchpotch of five persons who just happened to take off for whatever reasons we've taken off. But I'm proud of us. What we've achieved and survived.

LEWIS. Not survived it all yet eh?

PAUL. Well on the fervent hope we make it through this last leg alive, I'll be proud to sail into Whitby with you all. Whatever other people have to say about it.

LEWIS. Even the bishop?

PAUL. Ooh, yes, I don't know what the bishop's going to make of it but, still.

PAT. Thank you Paul.

EDNA. Amen! I think that deserves a toast. To the crew of the *Helga Maria*.

PAUL. To the crew.

PAT. To the crew.

LEWIS (*good natured*). Yeah yeah.

The sound of helicopters and the press.

Scene Two

The DOT Are Waiting

BRENDA *gives a press conference.*

BRENDA. I can confirm that the *Helga Maria* has been sighted in the North Sea and is being closely monitored on its course back to Whitby. We cannot yet confirm who the crew are or if they are all present for this return journey but I guarantee we will be speaking to Jack Lammiman and once he's within our waters, he shall not escape British justice.

Scene Three

Healing Up

PAUL *speaks into his Dictaphone as the crew sail home through calm waters.*

PAUL. August the twenty-first. We're about thirty miles south of Iceland. What a joy it is to have tea again. A real cup of tea now we've restocked the stores.

LEWIS *takes over from* PAUL. *Who moves to the bow, a new watch.*

August the twenty-second. Lots of young gulls swooping about the boat and trawlers, other signs of life. We're definitely about to rejoin the world after all these days cut off in the rugged purity of the Arctic wilderness.

A new day, a new watch.

August the twenty-third, picking up lots of chatter on the radio now and Jack's been on to Sunny again on the ship-to-shore, trying to get the lie of the land about things in Whitby. We hear that a reporter has chartered a boat to try and find us and there are fourteen countries out looking for us! Ooh I don't know. I think Jack's regretting the fact he's so strong-headed in everything in terms of coming and doing it illegally. He said he can go along with things so far and then he's his own man, he won't be pushed any more. So this Department of Transport, they can do what they will with him.

Projection: 'August 24th. Day 25.'

It's smooth sailing. JACK *is at the wheel.* PAUL *brings him a mug of tea. Silence for a time.*

JACK. How's the rib?

PAUL. Healing up.

JACK. You'll be pleased to be home I'm sure.

PAUL. Yes and no, I think? Starting to think I'll miss all this. I certainly feel the spell it casts.

JACK. Good. I'm glad of it.

Below deck, EDNA *hands* LEWIS *a note.*

EDNA. Here. Don't look so surprised, or are you not used to girls giving you their phone number?

LEWIS. Good one.

EDNA. We could always use a good tenor. Never enough male voices in the Whitby Players. There was talk of doing *Pirates of Penzance* for the autumn show and we are real pirates now aren't we so, you'd be a shoo-in for a soloist.

LEWIS. You're a case, Edna.

EDNA. I do hope you'll try and see your fiancée –

LEWIS. I got a feeling she won't be me fiancée no more, you know.

EDNA. No. But she at least deserves an explanation. And the chance to tell you you're a pig to your face.

LEWIS. Lovely.

EDNA. Look, pegging it off to the Arctic's a bit extreme as jiltings go –

LEWIS. Well if a job's worth doing!

EDNA. Now one more thing you: I have a spare room. And odd jobs that need doing. Should you ever need a bed, don't go sleeping in the harbour.

LEWIS *gives* EDNA *a little peck on the cheek.*

PAUL. You know, it's been far from perfect, it's been, completely mad to be honest but you have given us all something rather wonderful. I mean who else would have brought us on all this trip? This motley crew!

JACK. You certainly are that. Well, given you a few new stories for your sermons at least.

PAUL. Quite! I got my sea legs, got my 'Blue Nose' certificate and I've been into the wilderness... I don't know yet, I don't know what any of this means but, I will in time. I have faith.

JACK *is touched. He pats* PAUL *on the shoulder.*

Will I see you back in church Jack?

JACK. If I'm not in prison.

Scene Four

A Hero's Welcome

The sound of seagulls and crowds. EDNA *rings the bell.*

EDNA. Land ho!

Projection: 'Day 27. Whitby.'

PAUL, EDNA, LEWIS, PAT *and* JACK *stand on the main deck as they sail toward Whitby Harbour.* EDNA *wears her hat.*

JACK. Here we go. From the snows and the mountains of the Arctic to a blinking heatwave in Whitby!

PAT. Cor no more need for the woollen jerseys!

PAT *takes her woolly jumper off. They blink into the sunlight.*

PAUL. What a thing to come back on a bank holiday!

LEWIS. Why did I let you nutcases talk me into this.

EDNA. Ooh where's your sense of adventure!

PAT. Are all these chaps here to escort us?

EDNA *starts waving.*

EDNA. It's our flotilla! At last!

JACK. Well, it's been on the front page, they want to know the amount of blood going to be spilled I think.

LEWIS. It's like the guillotine you know. All the old women sitting round with knitting needles counting the heads coming off.

JACK. Thank you Mr Turnbull. Such a good friend, he comforts me to the end!

I have a feeling they'll let us off. That aircraft that overflew us two days ago. It could have picked us up.

The sound of huge crowds cheering. They're amazed.

EDNA. They're cheering us home! Oh Jack, they're cheering for us!

LEWIS. This isn't for us, there must be something else happening.

PAUL. There's Ruth and the girls! Oh my girls!

PAT. We made it.

LEWIS. So this *is* for us?!

EDNA. Whitby we love you! Wave! Everyone wave!

PAT. I hate waving, it's so inane.

LEWIS. Smile there's photographers and all.

EDNA. Where's my lippy? Oh my hair must be a fright. I knew it made sense to bring the hat!

Fireworks explode above them.

PAUL. This is incredible.

LEWIS. There's the bishop.

PAUL. Where?

LEWIS. Oh he looks furious, he's shaking his fist –

PAUL. Very funny.

JACK. Well done everyone. Stand by to dock.

As the Helga Maria *docks and the crew disembark, the clamour of the crowd is overtaken by a hungry press pit and the click and flash of many press photographers all crowding around* JACK.

PRESS (*voice-over*). Rebel returns home to hero's welcome! In an entrance that was as much theatre as it was navigation, the rebel skipper who led authorities on a merry three-thousand-mile dance to the Arctic Circle sailed back into Whitby to a hero's welcome after evading fourteen navies and three air force –

PRESS 2 (*voice-over*). It is, and remains, a wondrous story of English heroism. It stars Jack Lammiman – a middle-aged pleasure-boat operator, a Yorkshireman whose adventures evoked the amateurish bravado of Scott of the Antarctic, the buccaneering style of Drake and the accident-prone dash of Eddie 'The Eagle' Edwards!

PRESS 3 (*voice-over*). Lammiman, sixty-three, could face a maximum fine of fifty thousand pounds and up to two years in prison yet he seems as resigned to his fate as he is unrepentant.

JACK. I fully expect to go to jail but I shall be the only man prosecuted for sailing to the Arctic without fire buckets.

PRESS (*voice-over*). The *Helga Maria*, dubbed 'an old tub' is being impounded by the Department of Transport with immediate effect.

The former crew disperse. The sound of heavy rain.

Scene Five

Friends Reunited

Projection. '1992. Whitby Magistrates' Court.'

A dim and drizzly day. SUNNY *and* EDNA *wait under an umbrella.* PAUL *spots them and heads over.*

EDNA. Paul! Coooee! Over here!

PAUL. I was worried, I was late.

SUNNY. No you're alright, we've got a few minutes yet.

PAUL. Where's Jack?

SUNNY. In t'cells.

EDNA. Isn't it dreadful?

PAUL. Innocent until proven guilty I thought.

SUNNY. I spose he is under arrest.

PAUL. Isn't it a horrible irony? All his talk of freedom…

SUNNY. We should go in –

EDNA. Just a few more minutes. I was so hoping we could go in, all together. Only seems right doesn't it? Do you know if they're coming?

PAUL. I left a message for the last place Lewis was staying but, you know what he's like, disappeared into the wind again and I'm afraid all this movie stuff has rather put people's backs up.

SUNNY. Oh don't. I'm not dealing with it no more. I said to Jack, I said 'I don't know what to do with these Hollywood people come calling you need to get a bloomin' agent' so you'll never guess who he's got. You know Brian from Marwoods – the estate agents?!

PAUL. The estate agents?

SUNNY. Yeah. He's taking the calls and all! Least they're not bothering me up at Greendales.

EDNA. You know what the producer said to me – there's no place for 'elderly ladies' in this movie – Pat and I 'elderly ladies'?! Mature perhaps, but never 'elderly'! I said excuse me, you tie a half-hitch to mend a broken stern line in a force-six gale on a four a.m. dog watch and get back to me on who has 'a place in this story'!

PAUL. I shan't be in it either. 'It's Jack's story' they told me, as if he was the only one that sailed there, all alone.

LEWIS (*off*). Ahoy ya salty dogs, youse all got soft eh!

LEWIS *strolls over to join them.*

EDNA. Lewis!

PAUL. Good to see you mate!

LEWIS. Where's the paparazzi? I've only come to try and cop off with a page-three bird.

PAUL. How are you keeping?

LEWIS. Upright most days.

EDNA *hugs* LEWIS *and then cuffs him around the head playfully.*

EDNA. Oh I've missed you and I've been worried, you're so utterly dreadful at keeping in touch!

LEWIS. Treat 'em mean, keep 'em keen. You know that, you man-eater.

SUNNY. We really should go in.

EDNA. Did you miss us?

LEWIS (*calls*). Like a hole in the head. Get a shift on Pat!

PAUL. Pat's here?!

LEWIS. Just paying for parking.

(*Calls*.) You minting that money yourself, get a shift on girl!

EDNA. Oh how wonderful!

PAUL. You came together?

PAT *hurries to join them.*

LEWIS. Yes, just telling them about our torrid affair my darling. It's all out in the open now.

PAT. Must you be so vulgar? Hello everyone.

LEWIS. She's obsessed with us.

PAT. I saw this poor bedraggled wretch hitch-hiking on the outskirts of Scarborough and most ill-advisedly gave him a lift.

SUNNY. Come on, it's almost nine.

They head inside the court.

LEWIS. Hey Paul, d'ya get a kicking off the bishop or what?

PAUL. He said it was 'light relief' actually.

EDNA. You're looking very tanned Pat.

PAT. I've just got back from Tahiti.

EDNA. Tahiti?! What was that a package thing?

PAT. No, I sailed there Edna.

EDNA. You sailed to Tahiti?!

PAT. Yes, of course. What have you been doing – sitting around knitting?

PAT *swans into the court.* EDNA *races after her.*

EDNA. Urr no actually! 'Miss Tahiti.'

Scene Six

Jack in the Dock

The trial. JACK *stands in the dock in court. The sound of*
a MAGISTRATE *banging their gavel.*

MAGISTRATE (*voice-over*). Mr Lammiman you stand accused
of breaching forty-three separate offences as detailed by the
Department of Transport under the Merchant Shipping Act
including sailing in defiance of a detention order, sailing in
a vessel with significant safety issues deemed unfit for
purpose and unlawful transportation of civilian passengers
into international waters causing danger to life.

EDNA. What nonsense!

PAUL. Shhh Edna.

MAGISTRATE (*voice-over*). Order.

EDNA. We're all here in one piece aren't we?!

PAT. Edna –

EDNA. Well aren't we?! He'll tell you and he's a vicar!

MAGISTRATE (*voice-over*). Order!

LEWIS. Shoulda brought popcorn for this.

MAGISTRATE (*voice-over*). The state calls to the bench
Captain Brenda McCawlee with an official statement on
behalf of the Department of Transport.

BRENDA *gives testimony.*

BRENDA. Thank you Your Honour. Much has been made in the
press over the last few months of the rebel outlaw 'Captain
Jack Lammiman' and even that is where the misconceptions
start. 'Captain Lammiman' has no recorded marine
qualifications except the University of Life. According to
legal statutes he's not qualified to be a deckhand let alone
a captain, no matter what he calls himself. It's easy – and in
some quarters tempting – to make Jack Lammiman into a folk
hero. The little man who battles against unnecessary
government bureaucracy 'his only crime was sailing to the
Arctic without fire buckets'. 'The ship's bell was two
centimetres too small.' That is true. On our last recorded visit

the ship's bell was two centimetres too small. The ship's whistle was as old as the ship, sixty-two years old.

The distress flares were expired, rope frayed beyond use to give just two examples in a list of other vital safety measures either wholly missing or else found of substandard quality.

In my own personal opinion, I have no doubt of Mr Lammiman's sailing prowess or skill.

The completed voyage of just under three thousand miles is a testament to that in itself. However, the same cannot be said for the crew of the *Helga Maria*. Officially, the schooner should have been sailing with a qualified master and three deck officers – not with seventy-two-year-old Patricia Stubbs, who had only taken up sailing at the age of sixty. A Mr Lewis Turnbull whose address, relevant qualifications and whereabouts we have been unable to ascertain. Seventy-three-year-old Edna Whelan and the forty-three-year-old Reverend Paul Burkitt, neither of whom had much experience beyond day trips in the harbour. I suggest to the court that this voyage of 'plucky rebels' could have so easily ended in wholesale tragedy and the fact it did not is more due to luck than to anything else.

Due to Mr Lammiman's reckless disregard for life it is the opinion of the Department of Transport that the court bring to bear the fullest sentence it is possible to hand down.

MAGISTRATE (*voice-over*). Thank you Captain McCawlee. Mr Lammiman, do you have any comment before we adjourn to consider sentencing?

–

Mr Lammiman?

JACK. I'm just a square, bog-standard, normal sort of sailor. I believe in law and order. But the law is not to be taken by the letter. Otherwise, we'd have plain-clothes policemen watching us dropping litter. And I'm talking like William Scoresby would talk. I did what I did and I'm guilty of it, but I leave it other people to draw their own conclusions.

The sound of ocean swell. JACK *disappears.*

Scene Seven

Sunny Sums Up

SUNNY *leaves the court in the rain and turns to us.*

SUNNY. So that was that. Hiya, it's me, Sunny. Jack ended up
with a thousand-pound fine and then four days in prison for
not paying that fine. The man who never wanted an anchor
ended up in prison, it's dead ironic. And they made this
movie *Captain Jack* it were called. And all the press and all
the hoo-ha, it were all about Jack, Jack and more Jack. Thing
is, by the time the bloody movie were being made he were
halfway across the Atlantic Ocean. On a voyage that nearly
killed a whole other cast of folk. Brownie's honour. It's all
true! But what about this lot?

*Projection: For the first time we see original photos of the
crew of the* Helga Maria. *We hear the real recordings from*
PAUL*'s original tapes. The tape whirrs forward.*

PAUL (*recording*). I mean we're on the verge of an
international incident now which is quite incredible.

PAT (*recording*). My name is Pat Stubbs and I live in Cornwall
and I came up to Whitby on Monday and have stayed two
nights aboard this ship. It is an unusual ship.

EDNA (*recording*). My expectations of the trip are an
adventure, it's all unknown to me...

Epilogue

PAUL, EDNA, PAT *and* LEWIS *leave the court. It's still raining. As the others bicker,* PAUL *lights a cigarette, lost in thought.*

EDNA. That wasn't a trial, that was a farce? Wasn't it a farce?!

LEWIS. No, it's brought it all back. I been saying it was mint but now I'm counting up the ways I could've died. There's a lot of 'em.

PAT. I hate to agree with Lewis –

EDNA. Oh you love to agree with Lewis, it's like being back in the mess.

PAT. I'm just saying it is rather alarming, we had no idea –

LEWIS. Seventeen. I can think of seventeen distinct ways we could have all died.

EDNA. And yet we prevailed!

LEWIS. I need a drink.

EDNA. Oooh yes.

EDNA *puts her arm through* LEWIS*'s.*

PAT. Very wise. Paul? You have the strangest expression.

PAUL. I was just trying to work it out – if I could go back, knowing everything I know, would I do it all again? I mean, what's my excuse, I wasn't a sailor, hadn't sailed anywhere before except for chugging along a few feet on my houseboat. So why did I sail to the Arctic on Jack's say-so? It was dangerous, it was reckless, it was absolute chaos but... I'd do it all again. In a heartbeat. I know in my bones that I would. Wouldn't you?

LEWIS. No.

EDNA. Liar.

Oooh, it was the most glorious fun though wasn't it?

PAT. I don't know about 'fun' but it certainly was an adventure.

They look to one another and share a knowing smile of acknowledgement.

PAUL. You know what it is? It's a melody I've carried with me all my life, a faith. An insatiable faith in life.

'Freedom! '90' by George Michael.

Curtain.